HOW TO SUCCEED
IN ~~BUSINESS WITHOUT~~ *ANYTHING BY*

REALLY TRYING

LYMAN MacINNIS

Random House Canada

Random House Canada and colophon are trademarks.

www.randomhouse.ca

Library and Archives Canada Cataloguing in Publication

MacInnis, Lyman, 1938–
How to succeed in anything by really trying / Lyman MacInnis.

ISBN 978-0-307-35724-3

1. Success in business. 2. Career development. I. Title.
HF5381.M262 2008   650.1   C2008-903624-7

Jacket and text design: Terri Nimmo

Printed and bound in the United States of America

10 9 8 7 6 5 4 3 2 1

This book is dedicated to Lauren Grace MacInnis,
the newest member of the clan

CONTENTS

INTRODUCTION

A number of years ago, a fellow by the name of Shepherd Mead wrote a best-selling book titled *How to Succeed in Business Without Really Trying*. The book was actually satire disguised as a self-help guide. A couple of Broadway producers, Abe Burrows and Frank Loesser, turned it into a long-running musical on Broadway. It not only was a stage hit in London, but also had a popular Broadway revival a few years after its original run. Altogether the show had a total of 2,485 performances. It was even made into a hit movie. So it's not surprising that the book's title has endured to this day as an ironic catchphrase for undeserved achievement.

However, Mead's book was satire. This book is the real thing. It will show you that anyone can achieve success provided they define it in reasonable terms and strive for it with the right mental attitude. This book will also provide you with a framework for reaching your potential. But, as the title implies, its premise is that you're not likely to succeed without really trying.

As a matter of fact, you're not likely to succeed without trying really hard.

Any success achieved without really trying is better characterized as luck, but even at that, luck is usually some sort of opportunity meeting some sort of preparation. To win the lottery you have to buy a ticket.

It's not surprising that people want to be successful in the things they do. What is surprising is the number of people who don't fully understand what constitutes success. Equally surprising is the number of people who don't know the steps to take in order to achieve it. This book will clarify both for you.

Look up the word "success" in the dictionary and you'll find a definition such as "a favourable result." But, in any particular endeavour, success usually means more than that; it's either a specific favourable result or the culmination of a series of favourable results.

Success can be described in many ways. Someone once wrote that success isn't where you are, but rather the distance you travelled to get there. That's certainly one measure of success, but to thoroughly measure the degree of success achieved in the distance travelled, you also have to factor in the obstacles overcome along the way.

Someone else said that success is doing what you like to do and getting paid for it. That's a cute definition, but even though you may love your work as a middle manager, if you have the capability of being a vice-president and would like to be, you're still a work-in-process on the road to success.

Many people consider any major achievement to be a success. Although that is true as far as it goes, a major achievement is usually a long-term success that is the result of achieving over time a series of short-term successes. Consider, for example, an aspiring young athlete for whom playing professionally equals success. Along the way to this long-term success he will have to achieve many shorter-term successes that contribute to the ultimate goal, such as scoring a championship-winning home run, touchdown, or goal; moving up through the minor leagues; playing injury-free seasons; and being drafted by a professional team. Even if he reaches his goal of becoming a professional athlete, his definitions of success will have to be reset to include achievements such as winning a scoring title or playing on a championship team.

If you're a busy executive assistant, a short-term success might simply be having fewer items on your to-do list when you leave for home in the evening than were on it when you arrived at the office that morning. A successful day could also be one in which you managed to eliminate a particularly onerous and vexing item from the list. But your long-term success target might well be moving into your boss's job.

As a parent, success today might be convincing your teenagers to do their homework, but a few years from now success would be seeing them graduate with honours. After that, their successes could include finding good jobs, marrying compatible spouses, having children, and so on.

Success has many definitions because it usually means different things to different people; it can even mean different things to the same person at different times. A thousand-dollar sale might qualify as a great success to a sales trainee, but two years later, the same sale made by the same person, now a seasoned veteran, would probably be just a routine event and not considered a success at all.

Still another reason why the definition of success can be elusive is that it's not a static condition. It may exist in various forms for a very long time, such as a long and steady climb up the corporate ladder to the top job in your organization, or it may last for only a fleeting instant, such as a hole-in-one.

Some pertinent examples of success that have always impressed me are

- adequately dealing with a problem. Any time you adequately deal with a problem you have enjoyed a short-term (and sometimes long-term) success;
- being able to tolerate insecurity, like any coach in professional sports;
- pushing on after a setback, another example of a

short-term success necessary to achieving your long-term success;

- accomplishing something you were determined to do rather than something that you were destined to do, such as starting your own successful business rather than inheriting the family firm;
- knowing that you did the very best that you could, which should always be considered a success;
- doing today what someone else is planning to do tomorrow, yet another short-term success on the road to greater achievements.

Although success can have many meanings, one constant is that success is always personal. Whatever you're doing, and wherever you're doing it, the opportunity for success is always there. It can be found at home, at work, at play, at school, and in all your relationships. Success is the reward you get for doing your absolute best, which is usually completely within your control. Although you can sometimes fool other people, you can't really fool yourself. No matter how things look to others, you will always know whether you're truly succeeding because you will always know whether you're doing your best to reach your potential. It's worth noting here that, in the context of this book, reaching your potential is not just about winning in a competitive sense; it also includes achieving a satisfactory level of performance within the reasonable bounds of possibility.

It's important to never measure success by comparing yourself with someone else. Unless that other person's personal circumstances are identical to yours (and it's not likely that they are), you're comparing apples and oranges. Another reason you shouldn't measure your success by comparing yourself with others is that, even though you may not realize it because you don't know their true potential, they, by not doing their very best, may be failing.

In addition to the elements of achieving success described in each chapter of this book, there are four overriding considerations to keep in mind:

- You can't sit back and wait for things to happen; you have to make them happen.
- Having the will to succeed is important, but having the will to prepare is essential.
- A setback is not a failure unless you quit.
- No amount of success at work can compensate for failure at home.

During my career, I've dealt extensively with very successful people from all walks of life, from fledgling entrepreneurs to CEOs of Fortune 500 companies; from greenhorn athletes and entertainers to internationally renowned superstars; politicians; and ordinary solid citizens.

I've seen a great deal of success and some failures.

What I've learned is in the following pages.

BASIC TOOLS
AND
FUNDAMENTAL STEPS

There are two basic tools and three fundamental steps involved in achieving success in any particular endeavour. The basic tools are knowledge and skills, and the three fundamental steps are

- identifying the knowledge and skills needed to achieve the success you are seeking;
- realistically assessing the level of knowledge and array of skills you already possess;
- acquiring the knowledge and developing the skills that you lack.

Let's begin with the first of those two basic tools: knowledge. You acquire knowledge through study, experience, and being around people who know more about something than you do. All three methods are useful, but the one that's most efficient, and most under your control, is study.

Reading is to the mind what exercise is to the body.

People who don't read are no better off than people who can't read. When he was a young man, even though he had to walk many miles to and from the nearest library, and had to read by candlelight when it was dark, Abraham Lincoln stayed up late reading every night. When asked why he went to so much trouble to read so many books, his reply was, "I will study and get ready; perhaps my chance will come." Even as a very young man, the future president instinctively knew that one of the key elements in achieving success is the acquisition of knowledge.

At least one-quarter of your reading should be out-side your field of work. This will broaden your horizons and make you a better-informed and more interesting person. Knowledge is rarely wasted. If nothing else, the more you know, the less you'll be surprised. Sometimes it's the things you don't know that keep you from being successful, and sometimes it's thinking you know some-thing when you really don't that's the problem. The more you read, the less you'll encounter these problems. It's also useful to remember that the next best thing to knowing the solution to a problem is knowing where to find it. A few years ago my firm wanted to put on a business development seminar for partners and senior staff. We were a bunch of accountants and consultants, not salespeople, and this was back before professional services firms had sales and marketing departments. We didn't even know what aspects of sales and marketing the seminar should cover, let alone who should lead it. But I remembered a book I had read a couple of years before entitled *The 5 Great Rules of Selling*. By referring back to this book I was able to determine a general idea of what we needed and was able to contact the author.

And since you can't learn everything in the library or on the Internet, try to learn something from every experience, keeping an eye open for better ways to do things and always considering why particular results, either good or bad, occur. If you aren't already an observant person you need to become one. By paying attention to everything that's going on around you, you'll soon discover that there's really no such thing as an uninteresting subject, just uninterested people. Until you fully understand something that may be important to your success, be completely open-minded about it; become interested before you become judgmental. The person who knows *how* something is done may get a job, but the person who knows *why* it's done in a particular way will be the boss.

The most overlooked method of gaining knowledge is taking advantage of being around people who know more about something than you do. Pay attention to what they do and say. Although you should do more listening than talking, don't be afraid to ask questions. Even though there are sometimes stupid answers, there actually is no such thing as a stupid question. Never put a limit on your curiosity; when you're curious, ask.

An excellent way to combine both study and being around people who know more about something than you do is to take courses dealing with subjects that will be useful in reaching your potential. But don't just be a passive auditor of a course. Get involved. Ask questions. Make suggestions. Even if you have to stay late to discuss it with your instructor, try not leave a session unclear about anything that was covered.

When pursuing any of these means of gaining knowledge, it's important to take notes of interesting observations, facts, and statistics. It's equally important to develop a filing system that will allow you to refer to them easily. Don't be too quick to throw away any of these notes and observations. Even in this age of instant Internet data access, because you made your notes in a particular, and probably personal, context they will likely be more useful to you than generic information on the Web.

Two areas of knowledge that you should never stop developing are your vocabulary and your grasp of grammar. Being able to find the precise words, and being able to use them correctly, will always give you an advantage over others and will enhance your reputation as a person to whom attention should be paid. Any time you encounter a word that you don't know the meaning or pronunciation of, look it up in the dictionary at your first opportunity. You should take note of the various meanings, synonyms and antonyms listed for the word.

Many dictionaries are now available online, so for ease of access you could build your personal list of new words right on your computer. The next step is to make the new word part of your vocabulary by using it in conversation and writing. But always make sure your use of the word is appropriate; you don't want to come across as a pompous wordsmith. Doing crossword puzzles is another way to improve your vocabulary, as well as being a great way to relax.

Now let's turn our attention to the second basic tool of success: skills.

There's an adage that says, "Knowledge is power," the implication being that knowledge breeds success. The adage is wrong. It's not knowledge that's power; it's the *application* of knowledge that provides the power, which contributes to success. You've no doubt encountered knowledgeable, well-educated people who are not nearly as successful as they should be. The likely reason that these people haven't reached their potential is that they haven't acquired the necessary skills with which to successfully apply their knowledge.

A variety of skills is needed to apply knowledge in an effective, successful manner. For example, even after many years of university and medical school, well-educated, extremely knowledgeable graduates must still serve long and rigorous internships and residencies before they're allowed to practise on their own. The same holds true for lawyers and public accountants.

Would you ever consider going up in an airplane with a pilot who had studied all the textbooks and manuals, and even passed all the written examinations, but who had never actually flown a plane? Of course you wouldn't.

You must continually hone your existing skills by using them, while at the same time acquiring new skills that will be useful to you. Just as there are three ways to obtain knowledge, there are three ways to identify the skills you already possess (they may be latent, so you may not realize you have them) and to determine the skills that you need to acquire.

The first method is to objectively assess the things that you do well and also the things that you don't do well. But sometimes it's hard to be completely objective, so the second method is to ask others, such as colleagues, bosses, and mentors, for their assessments. Finally, and this is the method most often overlooked, you have to try new things and try doing old things in new ways.

The skills you need to acquire and develop are often evident in your surroundings. Ask yourself which skills would help you enhance the application of your knowledge, whatever you're going to be doing and wherever you're going to be doing it. For example, an engineer who has designed a new product and wants to get into sales in order to exploit it will need to take some sales training and improve his presentation skills.

But sometimes it's difficult to be objective about yourself and sometimes you simply won't know which particular skills you lack, so don't hesitate to ask successful people in your field to recommend areas for improvement. Your enquiries shouldn't be restricted to people with whom you work. An excellent way to meet more people from whom you can seek advice, as well as to broaden your horizons within your particular field, is to join trade and industry associations and to attend their conventions and training seminars.

Putting a limit on what you *will* do inevitably puts a limit on what you *can* do, so never put limits on trying new things or on doing old things in new ways. Not only might you discover one of those latent skills that you didn't realize you had, you also might identify a skill that you should, or would simply like to, develop. Every now and then, go somewhere you've never been before—especially in your imagination, by thinking about things you would like to try and places where you would like to go.

When you aren't improving, someone else is, and when you come up against that person, you will lose. Opportunities are never missed; the ones that you don't take advantage of, someone else will.

REMEMBER:
1. Success requires a combination of knowledge and the skills required to effectively apply the knowledge.
2. The three main ways to acquire knowledge are study, experience, and being around

people who know more about something than you do.

3. Reading is to the mind what exercise is to the body. Those who don't read are no better off than those who can't read.

4. The next best thing to knowing the solution to a problem is to know where to find the solution.

5. There's no such thing as an uninteresting subject; just uninterested people.

6. The adage "knowledge is power" is wrong; it's the application of knowledge that is power.

7. Putting a limit on what you will do puts a limit on what you can do.

8. When you aren't improving, someone else is, and when you come up against that person, you will lose.

9. Opportunities are never missed; the ones that you don't take advantage of, someone else will.

TO-DO LIST:

1. Read. And be sure that at least one-quarter of your reading is outside your field of work.

2. Maintain your curiosity, and when you're curious about something, ask.

3. Be observant; try to learn something from everything that goes on around you.

4. Be open-minded; become interested before you become judgmental.

5. Make notes and develop a filing system that will allow you to easily refer to them.
6. Continue developing your vocabulary and grammar.
7. Identify the skills you need to apply your knowledge.
8. Hone the skills you have and develop the skills you lack.
9. Try doing new things and doing old things in new ways.
10. Every now and then, go somewhere where you've never been before—especially in your imagination.
11. Ask successful people in your particular field to recommend areas for improvement.
12. Join relevant industry and trade associations and attend their conventions and training seminars.

BE EFFICIENT WITH THINGS, EFFECTIVE WITH PEOPLE

To succeed, you must be able to maintain successful relationships. It's fine to be efficient with things, but when it comes to dealing with people, you must be effective. You don't need to be a psychology major, but you do need to have a basic understanding of human nature in order to be a positive, motivating force. It isn't always easy, but it's always worthwhile. You start by understanding that there are three important factors that motivate people: they want to be respected, they want to feel appreciated, and everyone, at any particular time, has a prevalent train of thought.

Respect and appreciation are the main motivators of people, so it's axiomatic that to be effective with people, you must treat them with respect and seek ways to make them feel sincerely appreciated.

Because there are bound to be some people with whom you have to interact but don't particularly like, or for whom you have no feeling one way or the other, you may be of the opinion that treating everyone with respect and appreciation is insincere. It's not. Unless by their behaviour they have abrogated it, all people, simply by being living, breathing human beings, have the right to be treated decently; and the best way to treat people decently is to treat them with respect and show them appreciation.

When it comes to making people feel appreciated, there are three points to remember.

- You must be sincere.
- If you can't find some way to show sincere appreciation to a person, it's probably because you haven't looked hard enough. Look hard and you can almost always find something to praise. Maybe you have an employee whose work hasn't been up to par but who is always well-groomed and nicely dressed. The most effective way to deal with this person is to start by complimenting him or her on their appearance.
- If you really can't find some way to sincerely make a person feel appreciated, then do the second-best thing, which is never to treat them as if they're unimportant. Don't continually ignore the mail boy. Instead, always acknowledge him in some way, however small (preferably with a smile). You'll be glad you did the day you need someone to stay late to deliver your last-minute report.

The final motivating factor that needs to be understood is a person's prevalent train of thought. That phrase needs a definition: On any given day your prevalent train of thought is either the thing you find yourself thinking about most often during the day, or the thought that most often interrupts your concentration on something else. Sometimes your prevalent train of thought qualifies on both counts. For most people, most of the time, their prevalent train of thought is a preoccupying concern or worry. You have to remember that, just like you, every person you interact with is very likely dealing with some kind of problem, which could be as simple as a toothache or as serious as a critically ill loved one. And when a person's prevalent train of thought isn't a concern or a worry, it's probably something that he or she is looking forward to with great anticipation, such as leaving on a much-anticipated vacation.

There's not much you can do about another person's prevalent train of thought other than to remember that they have one, that it's highly unlikely it is the same as yours, and that it might be affecting their attitudes. A toothache could simply make the person you're dealing with a bit cranky, but the serious illness of a loved one could mean you can't get through to them at all. And there's not much point in talking to a person about something that needs to be done tomorrow when he or she is about to leave for ten days in the Bahamas.

Just as you judge people when you deal with them, they are, in turn, judging you. In dealing with people, you will be judged on four basic behaviours: what you say, how you say it, what you do, and how you do it, all of which are dealt with in detail in the following chapters. Most people have no problem understanding that they are judged on those four behaviours. But your understanding must go one step further by recognizing the four factors that influence other people's judgments of you: their intuition, their intelligence, their experiences, and their current emotional state.

About the only thing you can do regarding people's intuition is to recognize that it comes into play and always try to make as good a first impression as you possibly can. When you're going to be interacting with people for the first time, try to find out as much as you can about them and their expectations, dress appropriately, and treat them courteously.

Always make sure that you never insult a person's intelligence, such as by talking down to them or making assertions that are patently absurd in the circumstances.

You take people's experience into account by dealing with them on a level commensurate with that experience. For example, you would craft a speech about the ten most common personal financial planning mistakes on a completely different level for an audience of seasoned investors than you would for recent university graduates.

Finally, although you may never know exactly what a person's prevalent train of thought is, and therefore can't be sure of his emotional state, you should always be aware of the possibility he is dealing with something that has nothing to do with you but is a concern to him. Watch for clues to a person's emotional state, such as body language, facial expression, and tone of voice. If there is any indication that his emotional state may be an issue, you have to make allowances for it.

REMEMBER:
1. Respect and appreciation are the main motivators of people.
2. Everyone, at any particular time, has a prevalent train of thought that may well affect your dealings with them.
3. You are judged in four ways: what you say, how you say it, what you do, and how you do it.
4. When people are judging you, they are influenced by their intuition, intelligence, experiences, and current emotional state.

TO-DO LIST:
1. Work hard at being a positive, motivating force around others.
2. Show sincere respect and appreciation for people.

3. Acknowledge people's intelligence and experience.
4. Take into consideration the possible emotional states of people you are dealing with.
5. Always make the best first impression possible.

WHATEVER YOU ARE, BE A GOOD ONE

There's a line in an old country song that earnestly exhorts people to "do what you do do well." There are two possible interpretations of this advice. One is that you should do *only* what you do well; the other is that *whatever* you do, you should do it well. The former interpretation can be dismissed. Doing only what you do well would mean never broadening your horizons by trying new things, thereby seriously limiting your potential. So the latter interpretation, that whatever you do, you should do it well, is the one that will enable you to achieve success.

The line in the song is a lyrical way of saying that you should make the most of your abilities by always doing the best you can, with what you have, wherever you are, and whatever you're doing. Not only will this approach work wonders in achieving success, but a job well done is one of life's most satisfying experiences. Think about it and you will be able to come up with many examples of the gratifying feeling of knowing that you've done something to the very best of your ability.

Here's a way to test this theory: The next time you're faced with a boring chore or an aspect of your job that you don't particularly enjoy, instead of just going through the motions, say to yourself that just this once you're going to execute the task to the very best of your ability. No complaining. No loss of concentration. Just dig in with enthusiasm and do it better than you've ever done it before, all the time considering possible ways to improve your effectiveness and efficiency. The result will amaze you. Use this approach with everything you do and over time the results will be positively staggering.

Consistently making the most of your abilities usually means the difference between standing still and achieving success. But, what's required to make the most of your abilities? First, as outlined in Chapter 1, you must continuously add to your store of knowledge and arsenal of skills, which is why, in this context, the line in the song cannot possibly be interpreted as meaning do only what you do well. But there's more to making the most of your abilities than just becoming educated and skilled. This is where making an extra effort comes into the picture.

Hard work without ability is a shame, but ability without hard work is a tragedy. You've all seen examples of it. There are the athletes with tremendous skill and ability, yet they never win a trophy nor do their teams ever win a championship. It's usually because these particular athletes don't consistently perform up to their potential and therefore never make the most of their abilities. In some cases, because they don't try to stretch their skills, their skills actually diminish instead of becoming sharper; by not using it, they lose it.

Then there are the bright young employees who don't put in that extra effort and don't get promoted, such as the technician who didn't keep up to date with changing technology and so was overlooked while someone else became department manager, or the lawyer who didn't develop his communication skills, so he didn't make partner. There are the students whose marks remain short of what they could be because not enough notes are taken in class; or if notes are taken they aren't reviewed, so scholarships are missed and grades failed simply because the students don't try hard enough.

Speaking of students, you've probably seen people achieve success beyond what the level of their formal education would suggest they were capable of. These are people who seem to have done extraordinarily well on so-called natural ability. It's often been said that natural ability without education will often result in more success than education without natural ability. Maybe so, but it's rare indeed for people to achieve lasting success without a concerted effort to make the most of their abilities, whether "natural" or acquired.

Many years ago there was a cartoon in Ripley's famous *Believe It or Not* series depicting an ordinary iron bar worth, at the time, about five dollars. The cartoon went on to point out that the iron bar made into horseshoes would be worth about twice as much, or ten dollars. Made into sewing needles it would be worth $3,285. If it was turned into balance springs for watches it would be worth a quarter of a million dollars, fifty thousand times its original value! Of course this analogy for the uses of an iron bar is outdated, but the cartoon's message still holds true. Abilities are just like a tangible raw material: they're worth only what you do with them.

By now you have probably gotten the message that hard work is a key ingredient of making the most of your abilities, but there's still more required. In the long run it's going to be the quality of your work, not the quantity, that will determine the level of your success; and the quality of your work is affected as much by your attitude as it is by your level of knowledge and skill, maybe even more so.

There's a story I came across a few years ago that illustrates the importance of attitude in the workplace. It involves two truck drivers, both of whom spent the day picking up cans of milk in the countryside and bringing them into town for the milk to be processed. One was a young driver, bored with his work and consequently usually crabby, widely disliked, and often in trouble with management. The other was an older driver who was always in a good mood, was greatly respected by everyone, and was never in any trouble with his bosses. One evening after parking their trucks, the younger driver asked the other how he always seemed to have a positive attitude. The older driver said, "You went to work this morning, but I went for a drive in the country." In the right job with the right attitude, hard work doesn't seem like work at all, and quality is more readily achieved.

Quality is never an accident; it's always the result of thought and effort. Whatever you are, be sure you're a good one. When you're average, you're as close to the bottom as you are to the top, so always strive to get better. It's equally important to remember, though, that you don't have to be the very best at something in order to be successful at it. As poet Henry Van Dyke once said, "the woods would be a quiet place if no birds sang but those that sang best." But you do have to do *your* best, and keep in mind that "good enough" is forever the enemy of "best."

Making the most of your abilities is usually the link between wanting something and getting it. One of the best ways to prepare for the future is to make the most of your abilities today, which, as we've just been discussing, means having the right attitude. People who consistently do a good job every day tend to get promoted, even if they are in what seems to be a mundane job. When people think that their work isn't important, quality deteriorates. But if a job wasn't important, it wouldn't exist. All jobs aren't equal, but they're all important in some way in the overall scheme of things. Treat your job as if it's important, and others will begin to think that it is as well. Your attitude and performance will be noticed and appreciated by those who matter.

Finally, people tend to judge themselves by their ambitions and what they think they can do, but others judge them by what they actually accomplish. You build your reputation by getting things done. People will forget how many tasks you started, but they will remember how many you finished, especially those that you did well.

If you want to reach your full potential, you have to make the most of your abilities by always striving for quality and constantly looking for ways to do things better. Whether you're delivering newspapers, running a Fortune 500 company, or doing anything in between, remember that Easy Street is a dead end.

REMEMBER:

1. A task done to the best of your ability is one of life's most satisfying experiences.
2. Making the most of your abilities usually means the difference between a stalled career and achieving success.
3. Hard work without ability is a shame, but ability without hard work is a tragedy.
4. Your ability is worth only what you do with it.

5. Quality wins out in the long run, and you can't achieve quality without the right attitude.
6. When you're average, you're as close to the bottom as you are to the top.
7. "Good enough" is the enemy of "best."
8. One of the best ways to prepare for the future is to make the most of your abilities today.
9. There's really no such thing as an unimportant job. If your job wasn't necessary, it wouldn't exist.
10. You can't build a reputation on what you're going to do, but you can build a reputation on what you accomplish.
11. Easy Street is a dead end.

TO-DO LIST:

1. Always do the best you can, with what you have, wherever you are, and whatever you're doing.
2. Treat your job as if it's important, and others will begin to see it as important as well.

MIND THE PITFALLS OF ADVICE

Another cartoon from a few years ago depicted two old gentlemen lounging on a dock watching an expensive yacht sail by. "You know," said one, "the reason I was never able to afford a boat like that was because I never took any advice from anybody." "That's strange," said the other, "the reason I was never able to have a boat like that was because I always followed all the advice I got from everybody."

They were probably both right. Advice, whether it's being given or taken, can be both necessary and risky. It's necessary because without considered advice we'd all waste a great deal of time making, discovering, and correcting unnecessary mistakes. It's risky because what worked for one person in a given set of circumstances at a particular time may not be appropriate for another person at the same time or for the same person in a different set of circumstances, or for either at a different time.

Good advice comes from striking the right balance between the dictates of necessity and the inherent risks of the situation. Before advice is acted on, both the advisor and the seeker must be aware of what the problem really is, what specifically needs to be done to solve it, and the possible risks involved. This requires comparing the existing circumstances to the experiences from which the advice is being drawn, and then making the necessary adjustments to accommodate any differences—and in most cases there will be differences. For example, consider two people with an identical amount of money to invest. The right advice about the types of investments they should make would depend on such factors as their ages, their risk tolerances, what other assets they have, their liabilities, and their cash flow requirements. For example, although riskier investments might result in much higher returns, they would be inappropriate for older investors who can not afford to lose any of their capital and who need investment income to supplement their pensions; such investors would have greater peace of mind with lower returns from safe investments. On the other hand, a young executive earning a good salary might be unhappy with the lower return from safe investments and be quite willing to risk some capital for the chance of a higher, quicker return. When a proper balance is struck between the necessities and the risks of each person's situation, the possibility of that advice leading investors to success is considerably enhanced, and two people may end up with nice boats.

For ease of presentation, most of this chapter is cast in the form of *giving* advice. But, of course, when advice is being given, it's also being taken or rejected. So all of the aspects of advice discussed in this chapter should be considered and adjusted appropriately depending on whether you're on the giving end or the receiving end of the advice.

Before getting into the details of giving advice, I should mention some of the components of successfully receiving advice.

Quite often you won't know whether advice is good or bad until you've either followed it or ignored it and it's too late to alter the consequences. Therefore, you should always take into account the most important consideration in receiving advice, which is to determine whether the people who are giving it are competent to do so. If you don't already know, you will have to find out if their qualifications and experiences are appropriate in your circumstances. A person who gives financial advice to multinational corporations may be totally inappropriate to advise you on what you should do with a small inheritance. It's a fact of life that there are far more people ready to give advice than there are people qualified to do so. As my father was fond of saying, don't take carpentry advice from a guy with missing fingers.

It's usually a good idea to get more than one opinion if you can, and there will be times when advice simply shouldn't be followed. Because there are so many unqualified people eager to dispense advice (there's nothing sinister about it; it's just human nature), you should be wary of accepting advice that seems to be the exception to what most people are saying or doing. When evaluating the advice you receive, in addition to considering the qualifications of its source, decide whether your advisor followed the guidelines for giving advice that are discussed below.

The first point to consider when you're asked for advice is this: are you actually being asked for *advice*, or is it really your *help* that's being sought? There can be quite a difference.

If a colleague approaches you at work and asks for "advice" on how a project should be staffed, be sure you're not about to become the person who ends up having to juggle all of those employee assignments and schedules. Or, suppose a neighbour approaches you and asks for "advice" on building a deck on the back of his house. You'd better find out right away if you're being asked for some carpentry tips or whether you're about to be conscripted as a project manager for the next four weekends. Obviously, your response, and the consequences thereof, will vary widely depending on whether it's advice or help that's being sought. Any parent whose son or daughter has asked for "advice" on a school project has had hands-on experience with the difference between advice and help.

Once you've determined that it is advice that's being

asked of you, the next point to consider is the mindset of the seeker. Most people willingly accept and act on advice, no matter how valid it may be, provided it doesn't seriously interfere with what they were going to do anyway. So find out, as subtly as possible so as not to damage the spirit in which the advice is being sought and given, if the person asking is simply looking to reinforce a decision that they've already made or whether they genuinely want guidance and still have an open mind. If it's the former, and it's obvious that the chosen course of action is appropriate, then it's best just to agree with it. On the other hand, if the seeker has already decided upon a course of action that's clearly inappropriate, you'll not only have to apply all the rules of successful advice-giving, you'll also need a hefty supply of diplomacy and tact in order to allow the advice seeker to save face and willingly accept your advice. Many relationships have been damaged by the manner in which well-intentioned advice was offered or taken.

If you're unsure about either the mindset of the seeker or whether it's help or advice that's being sought, you have to probe. You have to ask questions, and lots of them. Never be afraid to ask questions, even if at first blush they appear to be stupid ones. As stated in Chapter 1, there may be an abundance of stupid answers but there really is no such thing as a stupid question. Asking what may seem like a stupid question is a lot less embarrassing than having to right a stupid mistake, especially one caused by your having given ill-informed advice. Experienced carpenters have an apt adage: measure twice and cut once (and those who do probably preserve all their fingers).

At some time in your life you've likely heard someone say, "I told him exactly what to do, and just look at what the stupid idiot did!" You've probably said that, or something similar, yourself. When advice gets messed up it's often, not always but often, the advisor's fault. When giving advice, it's not enough to speak (or write) in a way that can be clearly understood; you have to speak or write in such a way that you cannot be misunderstood.

The best way to do this is to remember that, just as a picture is worth a thousand words, one specific is worth a dozen generalities. Let's suppose you have a friend who asks you for advice on how to get a loan at the bank. Which of the following pieces of advice do you think would be more helpful?

a) Well, Sam, you'll have to convince them that you're credit-worthy, have a good solid reason for borrowing, show that you're going to be able to pay back the loan, and make a good impression.

or

b) Sam, draw up a list of your assets and debts and a simple budget of your income and expenses for the next year. Take those to the bank, tell the loan officer what you need the money for, and show how and when you will be able to pay off the loan. Also, Sam, dress well and be well-groomed, don't drop in wearing your gardening clothes.

If you've ever applied for a loan you'll know that (b) wins, hands down.

In order not to be misunderstood when giving advice, you have to speak or write in terms of the other person's interests and at their level of expertise. Remember that you probably know more about whatever it is you're talking about than they do, or else they wouldn't be asking for your advice. Use simple, clear, specific language that they will understand. What might be abundantly clear and perfectly understandable to you may be utterly confusing to someone else, and they may be too embarrassed to tell you that you're going too fast or that they have no idea what you're talking about. For example, inexperienced public speakers are often advised that when giving a talk they should "tell the audience what you're going to tell them, tell them, and then tell them what you told them." If it's left at that, the neophyte is very likely to just give her talk three times. The advice should be phrased something like this: Take a few seconds at the beginning of your talk to tell the audience in general terms what you're going to cover. Then give your detailed presentation, complete with appropriate illustrations and examples. Finally, close your talk by briefly summarizing your points.

Positive advice is a lot easier to take than negative advice. Find ways to accentuate the positive instead of dwelling on aspects you don't agree with. Don't say, "No, I don't think you should pull up stakes and move to Calgary, because you haven't really thought it through." Instead, say, "Relocating to Calgary may well be a good career move, but before making a final decision, here are a number of things you should look into." Then outline the areas you feel should be investigated further and, if possible, suggest ways for the person to do so. You'll also find that it's usually easier to be clear and specific when speaking or writing positively rather than negatively.

A client once asked me for advice as to whether he should leave a high-paying job with which he'd become bored to work as a full-time artist. He clearly had some talent for painting, but I wasn't sure that he had the discipline or the patience to make a living at it. The easy way out would have been to be negative and simply advise him against it. But that would have required me to admit my doubt that he had the characteristics required to become a full-time artist, which he might well interpret as a lack of confidence in his talent. The result, undoubtedly, would have been a loss of face on his part, damage to our relationship, and, knowing my client as I did, a hardening of his resolve to do what he had already pretty well made up his mind to do anyway.

Instead, I told him I thought he should look into it. However, I cautioned him that the safe way to approach his goal would be to keep his job until he knew more about whether there'd be a market for his work and whether he liked being a full-time artist. I pointed out that he could paint and sell his pictures in his spare time, at least until he had enough money saved to weather the dry spells that even established artists go through. He did just that. Now he works part-time and paints part-time. He's bored with neither. He sold his boat, not because he had to but because he'd rather be in the studio than out on the lake.

Advice that sounds good isn't necessarily good, sound advice. There are times when you have to recognize the obvious and refuse to be separated from common sense. If my client in the preceding example had little or no talent for painting, or was unlikely to ever be able to maintain a reasonable standard of living as an artist, I would have had to bite the bullet and tell him that I didn't think he should give up his job. Had this been the case, I would also have had to use a large dose of diplomacy and tact in order to maintain our good relationship. If you absolutely should say "no," then you must do so. But you should never say no without fully explaining your reasoning.

This raises another good point: if you're not equipped to give solid advice on a problem, recommend the seeker to someone who you know will be able to help. That's often the best advice of all. In the case of the executive who wanted to become an artist, I also had a client who owned an art gallery, and I asked him to look at some of the executive's paintings. The gallery owner's positive opinion was factored into my advice. If I hadn't personally known a gallery owner, I would have recommended that my client approach one himself to get an opinion on the merits of his work.

Most, if not all, of what's been said above applies whether the advice is being actively sought or is being dispensed gratuitously. However, when you discover that someone needs advice before she knows she needs it, extra caution is required.

People always resent having advice shoved down their throat, no matter how reasonable and beneficial that advice might be. People like to have their own ideas considered and respected, which, of course, is a basic human right to which we're all entitled, and which is part of the respect and appreciation mentioned in Chapter 2. The trouble is that logic alone seldom convinces those emotionally invested in their own way of seeing the world. A case in point would be people who, based on deeply held religious beliefs, prefer to face possible death rather than accept the advice of their doctors. In a battle between logic and emotion, emotion is usually the victor.

If your manner, tone of voice, or choice of words irritates a person, there's no way on earth they'll willingly accept your advice, no matter how well it's backed

up with illustrations, examples, and facts. Before gratu-
itous advice will be accepted, the potential recipient must
be in a receptive mood, both emotionally and intellec-
tually. So both the manner in which the advice is given
and the timing of the advice are critical to success.

The best way to achieve the right mood is to avoid a
superior attitude, let the other person save face, and be
positive, emphasizing what should be done rather than
what shouldn't be done. Work with the other person to
solve the problem and come up with the answers
together if you can. But, as mentioned earlier, be careful
not to end up doing the work yourself. Whenever possible, make sure the person you're advising understands
that whatever solutions you arrive at were at least partly
her idea too. This may take a lot of effort and a large
dose of patience, but the rewards, in terms of a positive
result and maintaining a relationship, are magnificent.

There are three times when you should never try to
give advice to anyone: (1) when people are tired, (2)
when they are angry, or (3) immediately after they've
made a mistake. It's also a pretty good idea not to give
advice when *you* are tired, angry, or have just made a
mistake.

Here's another important consideration when giving
or receiving advice: there are few things in life as bewil-
dering as the person who gives good advice but sets a
bad example. This is particularly true when applied to
parents. "Do as I say, not as I do" is the last refuge of

the advisor who lacks credibility. It's an admonition that seldom works with children and never works with adults. One of the best ways to enhance your reputation as a person who is worth listening to is to act on the advice that you give to others.

On the other hand, "Do as I say, not as I *did*" can be some of the most helpful advice of all. Having learned from a mistake is often the best qualifier for an advisor, and is always a powerful selling point when trying to change someone's mind. A good scare is a great teacher.

No matter how someone might phrase his request for your advice, the question that's really being asked is, "What would you do if you were me?" The operative words here are "if you were me." You're not really being asked what you would do "if you were you." You must translate "what *would you* do" into "what *should I* do." It is at this point that differences in circumstances and personalities, timing, and any other relevant facts have to be taken into consideration. What worked in one set of circumstances may not work in a similar set, even if only one minor factor is different. Circumstances are often similar but rarely identical, and personalities are *never* identical. As mentioned earlier, timing can be critical.

This doesn't mean that advice should never be given unless all details of the advisor's experience and that of the person being advised are identical, the relevant personalities are sufficiently similar, and the timing is perfect; far from it. What it does mean is that advice has to be tailored to suit the circumstances and personalities involved, and the timing has to be appropriate.

Given the choice, most of us would prefer basking in the sun on the deck of the yacht rather than on the dock.

REMEMBER:

1. Because circumstances are rarely identical and people never are, good advice doesn't come in one-size-fits-all.
2. The people who like advice the least are often those who need it the most.
3. It's usually best not to give advice until it's asked for.
4. It's never wise to give advice when you or the other person is angry or tired, or has just made a mistake.

TO-DO LIST:

1. Always determine what's being asked for, whether it's advice, help, or confirmation of a decision that's already been made.
2. To safeguard a relationship, always allow the other person to save face.
3. Be sure the advice fits both the person and the circumstances.
4. Ask enough appropriate questions to fully understand the situation.

5. Phrase your advice not just so that you can be clearly understood, but also so that you cannot be misunderstood.

6. Whenever possible, be positive rather than negative; but if "no" is the right word, don't be afraid to use it, provided you fully explain your reasons.

7. It's best to limit advice to that which you would follow yourself in the same circumstances.

8. When seeking advice, in addition to being sure the advisor is following the guidelines outlined in this chapter, be sure the advisor is qualified to give the advice.

HAVE A
WELL-STOCKED
SOCK DRAWER

Not many people react favourably when told to "put a sock in it." This euphemistic phrase is as offensive to most people as would be the more direct "shut up." But the reality is that "put a sock in it" can be pretty good advice when you are angry.

It would be naive in the extreme to suggest even the possibility, forget the probability, of going through life without ever becoming angry. There will always be situations that try your patience, and there will always be people who will severely test your ability to keep your cool. Success comes from controlling your anger, or at the very least minimizing the damage caused by what you say when your temper gets the better of you. Until you master this side of your behaviour, it's a good idea to have a well-stocked sock drawer.

Spouting off when angry will almost always cost you. The price you pay may take many forms, such as a damaged relationship, an ineffective communication, a missed opportunity, some lost income, or simply wasted time. Very rare indeed are the people who cannot trace paying each of these prices at least once because of losing their temper. And just as overspending at the store usually leads to an unhappy look at your bank balance after you get home, the price paid for speaking up when you've lost your temper is more often than not accompanied by later regrets.

So let's examine some ways to ensure that the socks can stay in the drawer.

The first step in curbing your temper is to know what triggers it. The second step is to recognize the warning signs. You then have to develop control mechanisms. The time-honoured practice of counting to ten before speaking or acting when angry is actually quite useful. When very angry it's probably a good idea to count to ten times ten, and you might want to take a walk around the block while you're doing it. But, since you might not always have that much time to cool down, there are some other things that you can do.

When you feel your blood pressure rising, ask yourself how much whatever it is that's causing it to rise will matter a year from now. It probably won't matter enough to warrant losing control of the situation in the present.

Another effective anger management technique is to think of the people whose respect you most want to keep (such as loved ones) and then act as if they are there with you. Of course, if it is one of the people whom you most respect who happens to be the target of your anger, then ultimate restraint is called for; that would definitely be a good time to take a walk around the block while you count to a hundred. Anger is always best vented in private.

Have you ever noticed that the angriest people are frequently those who know that they are wrong? Anger is often the manifestation of simply having no one else to blame. Remember that if you're right there's no need to lose your temper, and if you're wrong you can't afford to lose it. Because it's impossible to be poised and angry at the same time, much of what you say and do while angry is apt to damage your reputation and cause others to lose respect for you.

People's anger is often triggered by anger directed at them by others. One angry person is bad enough; two angry people are a recipe for disaster. When someone you're dealing with gets angry, it's time to end the discussion. Angry people usually don't cool down until either they blow off their head of steam or enough time passes for a natural cooling down to take place. Only after they've had the opportunity for their anger to dissipate should you try to reason with them. And it's never a good idea to direct your own wrath at an angry person. The problem with fighting fire with fire is that you usually end up with a lot of ashes.

Although it's often anger that gets people in trouble, it's usually pride that keeps them there. When regret sets in, whether it's right away or a week later, swallow your pride, sincerely and unequivocally apologize, and do whatever it takes to mend the fence. What I mean by "unequivocally" is to come right out and say, "I really regret losing my temper and I'm sorry I got angry with you." You'll gain a lot more respect by not beating around the bush. And avoid using weasel words such as "If I did (or said) something to upset you . . ." If you and everyone else involved know you're at fault—even if you're not the only one who is—shirking reponsibility will only worsen the damage to the situation and your reputation.

REMEMBER:

1. It may take years to build a relationship, but a single angry moment can destroy it.

2. When you're right, you can afford to keep your temper; when you're wrong, you can't afford to lose it.

3. What you say when you're angry may be the best speech you'll ever regret.

4. When someone you're dealing with gets angry, it's even more important for you to keep your cool.

5. Anger may get people into trouble but it's usually pride that keeps them there.

TO-DO LIST:

1. Use one or more of the following anger management techniques.

   a) It's old advice but it's still good advice: when angry, count to ten before speaking or acting; when very angry count to a hundred, and take a walk around the block while you do so.

   b) Act as if someone whose respect you don't want to lose is with you.

   c) Ask yourself how much whatever's upsetting you will matter a year from now.

   d) When regret about your anger sets in, whether it's immediately or a week later, sincerely and unequivocally apologize.

   e) If you must vent your anger, do it in private.

WIN ALL YOUR ARGUMENTS, LOSE ALL YOUR FRIENDS

Just as it's highly unlikely that you'll go through life without ever becoming angry, it's just as unlikely that you will go through life without ever having an argument with anyone.

Unless you're a hermit or a wimp, or have no principles whatsoever, you will inevitably find yourself in situations where you either have to defend your position or to try to change someone else's. Bullying supervisors, recalcitrant employees, totally unreasonable customers, insolent service personnel, and just plain obnoxious people exist, and when you encounter one of them, you may have to take a stand. It's called having the courage of your convictions, and if you don't have the courage of your convictions you're not going to reach your potential for success.

Even though having the courage of your convictions means you can't always *avoid* an argument, you can always *manage* it. To effectively manage an argument you must first know what you're talking about (everybody has a right to an opinion but no one should argue a position if he hasn't got his facts right) and then, as discussed in the last chapter, you have to keep a tight rein on your temper.

Some people dislike arguments so much that they think it is all right to remain neutral any time a contentious issue arises. They are wrong. The problem is that there's a difference between being neutral and being fair; and there are times when the only way to be fair is to take a stand. Although people who take a stand are sometimes wrong, people who never take a stand are always wrong, because when they do not stand up for what they believe in, they have, in effect, already made a bad decision. As I said, to be a successful person you have to have the courage of your convictions.

Imagine, for example, that you're in a meeting where a new company procedure is being hotly debated between two of your colleagues, both of whom you like and respect and neither of whom you would want to disappoint. Suppose you have some information that would clearly swing the argument one way or the other. In this case, remaining neutral by keeping quiet is not being fair to anyone. It's not fair to your colleague who would probably carry the day if you bolstered his case by divulging the information you have, nor is it fair to allow your other colleague to continue holding an erroneous position because you're withholding information. It's certainly not fair to the company if a wrong decision is made because of your so-called neutrality.

There's also the possibility that it will become known that you withheld information, which will do nothing for your reputation.

Situations in which being neutral isn't being fair arise at home as well as in the workplace. For example, assume you have a teenage daughter who is in some way taking unfair advantage of her younger brother. As a responsible parent you shouldn't remain neutral. To be fair, you have to take your son's side, thereby probably getting into an argument with your daughter; and as with any argument with a loved one, it is even more important for you to keep careful control of it, maintaining a reasoned discussion rather than allowing it to escalate into a family fight.

When dealing with children, it's often better to debate an issue in order to settle it than it is to settle it without debate. Debating with your son the issue of how much face piercing is appropriate will be far more effective in maintaining family harmony than just laying down the family law would be. You both may learn something, and you're also more likely to keep each other's respect.

As important as it is to have the courage of your convictions, it's equally important to not confuse courage of conviction with just plain stubbornness or, even more dangerous, with prejudice. It's been said there are only two types of people who never change their minds: dead people and fools. When you realize you're wrong, be willing to concede; when the other person admits that you are right, be easy to live with. Having a reputation as an "I-told-you-so" is never going to help you deal successfully with others. It's human nature for people whom you've annoyed to be on the lookout for opportunities to get back at you.

One indicator that you might be acting from stubbornness or prejudice, rather than from conviction, is that you catch yourself raising your voice. Another is that the other person is calmly making logical points that you can't calmly and logically rebut.

By definition there are at least two sides to every argument. It's always useful to remember that, when people argue with you, unless doing so out of spite, they aren't so much against *you* as they are *for* themselves. Depending on how biased people are, sometimes the only way to prove them wrong is to let them suffer the consequences of having their own way. Time sometimes makes more converts than reason.

It may happen that you suddenly find yourself in an argument when you least expect it, which usually means you're not adequately prepared to defend your position, so learn to recognize the omens. Body language and tone of voice can be clear harbingers of an impending disagreement. A jutting chin, glaring eyes, and clenched fists aren't signs that someone agrees with you, and when people say they "agree in principle" or "yes, but . . ." the argument is already under way.

Although the best way to win an argument is to be right, if you win all your arguments, you're going to lose all your friends. Be prepared to overlook what's not important. In matters of principle it's fine to stand like a rock in a stream, but in matters of taste it's usually better to go with the flow. For example, a manager should never allow an employee to hang a racially offensive slogan on the wall, but if the manager simply doesn't like a painting the employee has put up in his office, he or she should just keep quiet.

Although a disagreement doesn't necessarily have to cause personal problems between people, it often does. When you find yourself in an argument, try to keep the issue separate from the personalities. A very effective way to achieve this separation is to imagine that your best friend is the other person involved, and deal with that person as you would with your best friend, always remembering that hard arguments usually require soft words.

There are times when arguing is absolutely futile, the most obvious of which is when you are wrong. When you realize you're wrong, do as Dale Carnegie advises in *How to Win Friends and Influence People*: "admit it quickly and emphatically." State briefly what caused you to change your position and then move on. There's also no point arguing with confirmed bigots; they lower the argument to their level and then beat you with the experience gained by defending their position much more often than you've probably had to attack it. Nor should you waste time arguing with people whose opinions you don't respect, especially if they are clearly wrong, even though ignorance sometimes produces some very interesting arguments.

Avoid arguing with people who are angry; trying to change people's viewpoints when they're mad about something usually just results in the hardening of their positions.

As mentioned earlier, the best way to win an argument is to be right, but how you demonstrate that you're right is critical. The most effective way to prove that a stick is crooked is to place a straight stick beside it. Unfortunately, it isn't always that easy to prove your point, so to keep an argument manageable, you will need clear, logical, effective explanations and relevant illustrations and examples.

Even if what you say is beyond dispute, how you say it can determine whether the argument devolves into something worse. When trying to change people to your way of thinking, you'll not succeed by being disrespectful (especially by trying to demonstrate intellectual superiority) or by using a belligerent tone of voice. In addition to making your points in terms the other person can clearly understand and relate to, you need to use a conversational and non-challenging tone.

When it's obvious that an argument is about to start, or has already started, the most effective word in your vocabulary will be "why." Starting a sentence with "why" forces you to ask a question, such as: Why do you say that? Why do you feel that way? Why are you angry?

Such questions, asked in a conciliatory tone of voice, are often all that's required to defuse an otherwise explosive situation. It's also a marvellous way to learn something. Listen carefully, and as mentioned in Chapter 1, become interested before becoming judgmental (and this applies to both the issue and the people involved; always separate what's being said from who's saying it). When you sincerely try to understand other people's points of view, you'll be surprised how often they're honestly trying to do what they sincerely believe to be right.

An argument may have two sides but it also needs an end, and although it takes two people to start an argument, it only takes one to end it. A good indication that it's time to end an argument is when it has become long and drawn out. A long, drawn-out argument is usually a signal that neither side is going to prevail. Don't ever consider it a weakness to be the one to end an argument. If the need to get in the last word becomes overwhelming, use it to apologize for letting the discussion drag on for so long. When one person becomes angry, that's the time for the other one to put an end to the discussion. An effective way to do this is to say something like, "Look, we're obviously not going to resolve this right now. Let's leave it for the time being and discuss it later." Of course there would be nothing to be gained by adding "when you've cooled off," even though the matter shouldn't be taken up again until that happens.

To help prevent the recurrence of an argument, try to find out and correct whatever caused it in the first place. You'll often discover that it was just a simple misunderstanding, but there will be occasions when you simply have to, as the old saying goes, "agree to disagree."

If you want your life to be happier, remember this final piece of advice: when disagreeing with a loved one, deal only with the current situation; never bring up the past.

REMEMBER:

1. To effectively manage an argument you have to keep a tight rein on your temper.
2. There's a difference between being neutral and being fair.
3. People aren't so much against you as they are for themselves.
4. Sometimes letting people have their way is the only way to prove them wrong.
5. Win all your arguments, lose all your friends.
6. It's futile to argue with a confirmed bigot, a person whose opinions you don't respect, or an angry person.
7. The best way to prove a stick is crooked is to place a straight stick beside it.

8. The most effective word in an argument is "why" as in, "Why do you feel that way?"
9. Although it takes two to start an argument, it only takes one to end it.

TO-DO LIST:

1. When you're wrong, admit it; when you're right, be easy to live with.
2. Overlook what's not important.
3. In matters of principle stand like a rock in a stream, but in matters of taste go with the flow.
4. Keep issues and personalities separate.
5. To prevent the recurrence of an argument, find and correct whatever caused it in the first place.
6. When disagreeing with a loved one, deal only with the current situation; don't bring up the past.

NORMAN VINCENT PEALE CERTAINLY HAD ONE THING RIGHT

In 1952, Dr. Norman Vincent Peale wrote a book called *The Power of Positive Thinking*. It was on the *New York Times* best-seller list for more than three and a half years and over half a century later is still available in most bookstores. Although some of the book's contents proved to be controversial, the truth of the message in its title is indisputable. Positive thinking is indeed a very powerful force. Even doctors agree that a positive attitude probably contributes to longevity. (As a matter of interest, Dr. Peale lived to be ninety-five years old.) A positive attitude will definitely contribute to a more enjoyable and satisfying day-to-day existence, a condition that will undoubtedly contribute to success.

What you do can have a direct influence, often a considerable one, on many aspects of your life. You can influence your health by what you eat and drink, the amount of exercise you get, and whether you smoke. By acquiring the appropriate knowledge and skills, you can influence the type of work you do and where you do it.

But even health-conscious, very fit individuals are sometimes struck down by heart attacks, and it's not unusual for people to be forced to change jobs or job locations even when they don't want to. All of which goes to emphasize that the only aspect of life over which you have complete control is your attitude.

The level of your happiness or the depth of your despair is largely dependent on the degree of control that you exercise over your mental attitude. Bad luck and setbacks are an inevitable part of everyday life, but allowing yourself to be miserable about them is an option. Abraham Lincoln once remarked that most people were about as happy as they made up their minds to be. The choice really is yours. You can change your world by changing your thoughts.

We aren't born with our attitudes; we develop them. If you don't believe that being curious, positive, and happy about things is our natural state, take some time to closely observe children at play.

Consider, as a case in point, your work. If you're not happy in your job, you have only three choices: stay miserable, change your work, or change your attitude. No one should ever opt for continued misery, so if you're unhappy in your work you either have to change jobs or change your attitude. Even if a change of jobs seems to be the answer, you should examine whether your attitude needs to be changed as well. Otherwise you may end up simply being miserable in a different place.

Speaking of work, I once had a boss who told me that the three A's of a career are Ability, Ambition, and Attitude. He said that ability earns you your paycheque, ambition gets you your raises, and attitude usually determines the amount of both.

In any endeavour, whether professional or personal, things work out best for people who approach everything with a positive attitude, and the most important consideration in maintaining a positive attitude is to recognize that it is expectations that cause frustration. When your goal seems far away, think about a stonecutter who has to split off a slab of precious marble. He taps on his chisel fifty times with barely a crack showing. Then with the next tap of the chisel the piece splits smoothly and evenly. But it wasn't the fifty-first tap of the chisel that did it; it was that fifty-first tap *and* the fifty taps preceding it that did the job. The stonecutter didn't expect success at the thirty-first tap of the chisel, so when the slab didn't split then he didn't become frustrated and quit, but instead diligently carried on to ultimate success.

As pointed out in the first paragraph of this chapter, you can't always control circumstances. Nor can you always control what other people think about you and how they behave around you. But you *can* control your attitude toward both circumstances and people.

Circumstances can't get you down unless you let them. Instead of letting circumstances get the best of you, spend your time and effort putting together a list of things you can do to improve them. Similarly, people can't really make you disappointed, angry, or sad (or sometimes even happy, for that matter) unless you let them. When you feel your frustration mounting, remember the stonecutter and look first to adjusting your expectations.

A love of flowers will not make you a good gardener; you also have to be good at pulling weeds. So a sure way to improve your mental attitude is to get rid of the negatives in your life, just as you'd get rid of the weeds in your flower garden. Sit down and make a list of all the things that are causing you to have, if not a bad attitude, at least not a very positive one. Then objectively break down the list into two categories: those that are bad because of how you perceive them and those that are bad as a simple matter of fact. For the first category, change your attitude. When it comes to the second category, start by reminding yourself that you don't have to like facts in order to deal with them. But if they're weighing you down, you *do* have to deal with them. Instead of stewing about them or feeling sorry for yourself, ask yourself, "How can I improve this situation?" and then, with a positive attitude, decide on and take the necessary steps to do so. There's an old saying in Atlantic Canada that has relevance here: There's no such thing as bad weather, just inappropriate clothing.

No matter how tough things get, you'll deal with them much more effectively with a positive approach.

The difficulty of a task usually diminishes proportionately with the increase in your willingness to do it. A good way to improve your attitude in this context is to pick at least one thing each day that you've been putting off and then force yourself, without allowing negative thoughts to persist, to willingly deal with it. You can do for a few hours what it would appal you to have to do for a lifetime. Even easy tasks become difficult when done reluctantly. Raking leaves is not really a difficult job. But if you detest raking leaves, and will only do it reluctantly, it becomes a burden. Either hire someone to rake the leaves or change your attitude.

Attitudes are contagious, so don't be a carrier of bad ones. You have a clear choice as to how those around you will think about you and react to you. Every time you conduct yourself in a positive manner, you're influencing those around you in a positive way. Every time you act in a negative way, you're exerting a negative influence on those around you. Because attitudes tend to get reflected right back at you, being negative sets up a never-ending cycle of bad attitudes in which everyone, including you, is worse off than he or she would be in a positive-thinking environment.

As already mentioned, no matter how difficult things may seem, you'll do better with a positive approach, and the sooner you get started on it the better. I discovered a long time ago that if I can remain positive until about ten o'clock in the morning, the rest of the day will go a lot more smoothly. It's sometimes not easy, but it's always worthwhile. Dick Cappon is a good friend and a former partner of mine whom I've known for over forty years. I've never seen him be anything but upbeat, happy, and positive. I asked him once how he managed this. He said, "Well, when I wake up each morning I remind myself that I have a choice: I can make the best of this day or I can mess it up with a negative attitude. I always choose to make the best of it."

A really great attitude enhancer is to try to learn something from everything that happens around you and from everybody with whom you come in contact. Become sincerely interested in other people and genuinely curious about events, and your mind will become too positively occupied to allow bad attitudes to develop or frustration to creep in.

A very difficult time to maintain a positive attitude is when an important phase of your life ends: a loved one dies; children leave home to go out on their own; we're forced to leave a house and neighbourhood we love; even the loss of a pet can be devastating. When things like this happen, after you've shed your tears for what you've lost, remember to smile because you had it, and then be grateful for the things that you still have.

This is probably a good time to mention another great example of how important our attitude is. Four times during my life I've been awakened at night by telephone calls informing me that a family member has died. As a result, now when my phone rings at four o'clock in the morning and it's a wrong number, I'm never angry; I'm thankful.

It's a lot easier to develop and maintain a positive attitude if you are an enthusiastic person. It's hard to imagine succeeding in anything without having enthusiasm for it. As a matter of fact, people with less ability but more enthusiasm will usually outperform people with more ability but less enthusiasm. You can observe this dynamic in action at almost any sporting event, where enthusiasm makes ordinary athletes capable of extraordinary performances.

Whatever you are doing and wherever you are doing it, you will achieve a lot more if you approach it with enthusiasm. You will also enjoy doing it a lot more. If you can do something with genuine enthusiasm, you can probably do it forever.

Another positive aspect of enthusiasm is that it, too, is contagious. Enthusiasm tends to beget enthusiasm. With whom do you prefer to associate, enthusiastic people or dull, boring laggards?

Being human, we aren't always enthusiastic. But another good thing about enthusiasm is that if we *act* enthusiastic about something we tend to *become* enthusiastic about it, and fairly quickly, too. One of the best ways to become enthusiastic about anything is to set out to learn more about it.

Although you can never completely prevent negative thoughts from stealing into your life, you can definitely get better at getting rid of them when they do creep in. When you're grateful for all that's good in your life, better things follow.

One of the most misplaced expectations that we can have is to look to others for our happiness. Don't wait for someone else to make you happy; it may not happen.

REMEMBER:

1. The only aspect of life over which you have complete control is your mental attitude.
2. It's expectations that cause frustration.
3. A love of flowers will not make you a good gardener; you also have to be good at pulling weeds.
4. No matter how tough things get, you'll do better with a positive attitude.
5. Attitudes are contagious, so don't be a carrier of bad ones.
6. Enthusiasm makes ordinary people extraordinary.
7. If you can do something with enthusiasm, you can probably do it forever.
8. Enthusiasm may have to be faked, but never for long.
9. Although you can't completely eliminate

negative thoughts, you can get better at dismissing them.

10. Waiting for someone else to make you happy is a mistake; it may not happen.

TO-DO LIST:

1. Be positive until ten o'clock in the morning and the rest of the day will usually take care of itself.

2. Become interested in people and curious about events.

3. After you cry because you've lost something, smile because you had it, and then appreciate what you still have left.

4. When the phone rings at four in the morning and it's a wrong number, don't be angry; be thankful.

5. To become enthusiastic about something, learn more about it.

BEWARE THE ADDICTION

Without exception, over the long term, the most effective professionals and executives with whom I've been associated all had appropriately balanced lifestyles. And, yes, I did say *without exception* and the *most* effective. It's also been my experience, and again without exception, that workaholics, over the long term, are never the most effective people in any environment. Workaholics tend to eventually become narrow-minded, burnt out, unhappy, insensitive people who reach nothing close to their true potential. And a burnt out, unhappy CEO or managing partner is by no reasonable measure a successful person.

Don't get me wrong. All the successful executives and professionals I've known have indeed worked very long days and weeks, but they did it only when it was necessitated by circumstances. The extra hours were never worked because of blind ambition, lack of confidence, or trying to keep up with the Joneses. It is clear throughout this book that I passionately believe that hard work and dedication are necessary to succeed, but I also fervently believe that, as highlighted in the Introduction, no degree of success at work can compensate for failure at home.

A person's career shouldn't be his or her main source of self-esteem. Career satisfaction definitely should provide *one* source of your self-esteem (or else you're in the wrong field), but it should never be more important than the satisfaction realized from being a good spouse, a good parent, a good friend, a good neighbour, a good person to share a laugh with, and, when required, a good person to share a tear with. People should never base all their values on their jobs.

Anyone who consistently chooses work over a weekend at the cottage, a child's special event, a bridge game with friends, a quiet evening at home with a glass of wine and a good DVD, a nice dinner out with a special person, or taking the time to read a good book is heading for trouble—or worse, is already in trouble.

Work should never be a person's sole passion. No matter how dedicated to a career or profession, all people need to have outside interests that they feel strongly about and on which they regularly spend time. It's all the better if one of the interests is a hobby or avocation that requires the development and application of some non-work-related skill, such as painting, mechanics, woodworking, or playing a musical instrument. The narrowly focused workaholic is never as happy and, therefore, by definition, never as successful as the person with a number of varied interests. The person whose only tool is a hammer tends to treat everything like a nail.

Neither should work ever be your sole source of identification and recognition. As important as you may feel when you're introduced as "the person who was on TV talking about the economy the other night," or "the person who makes our IT department tick," it should be at least equally as satisfying to be introduced as "Ashley's dad," "Sammy's mom," or "the person who takes up the collection on Sunday." It's a major mistake to look solely to your job for fundamental emotional gratifications that are better provided by family, community, religion, outside interests, and friends.

As illustrated by the above examples, fundamental emotional gratifications should never depend on one relationship—especially if that one relationship is with your work. Your colleagues may be friendly and wonderful people to be around, but they shouldn't be your only friends and should never be surrogates for your family. If you're dependent on one relationship for your fundamental emotional gratifications, what happens if you lose that relationship?

It's not overstating the case to refer to this situation as an addiction. I know many people who consistently work eighty-hour weeks. I know people who will take a holiday only when forced to, and even then take their BlackBerries and a briefcase full of documents to the beach with them. I've been told of a partner in a downtown Toronto professional firm who slipped away from his wedding reception to go to the office for a couple of hours. But more telling, I've known far too many burnt-out, unhappy executives and professionals whose health, family, and personal relationships have suffered unnecessarily and often irreparably. I don't have the evidence, but I suspect there are people who worked themselves into an early grave—which is hardly justified by that bigger house and second car for which their widows no longer have any use.

So what do you do if you're in this trap? First of all, you and your family should have some serious discussions around setting your priorities. Next, you need to talk to your superiors at work. Then you have to decide what actions need to be taken. Some of these actions may be very difficult, such as lowering your standard of living or leaving your current place of employment, perhaps even changing your career. On the positive side, my experience has been that the necessary actions are rarely as difficult as they first seem to be. You'll probably find that your superiors will be more understanding than you ever thought they would be (and if they aren't, then that alone should tell you something about the choices you have to make). When you realistically assess the situation you'll also probably find that, if necessary, you and your family can actually be content with a less costly standard of living.

Taking action against workaholism always produces better results than anticipated, and the results of not taking action against this addiciton are always worse than expected.

REMEMBER:
1. The most effective executives and professionals have balanced lifestyles.
2. No degree of success at your workplace can compensate for failure at home.
3. Your sources of self-esteem, identification, and recognition should include family and friends as well your job.

TO-DO LIST:
1. If you're a workaholic, start taking steps immediately to rectify the situation.
2. If you're not a workaholic, be sure you don't become one.
3. Have passions other than your work.

THERE ARE FEW SHORTCUTS TO ANY PLACE WORTH GOING

People with clearly defined goals are potentially successful people, if for no other reason than because there's so little competition. Far too many people just plod along from one day to the next, not realizing that if they don't have a plan of their own, then their only hope is to be a part of someone else's.

Most people have some idea of what they'd like to achieve, but goal-setting consists of a lot more than merely thinking about what you would like to do and musing about when you would like to do it. It's like taking a long trip. You need to know your destination, have a pretty good idea of how to get there, estimate how long the journey is bound to take, and plan the stops you're going to make along the way. Anyone who's done this type of planning knows that there are few shortcuts to any place worth going.

To be effective, goals must be clear and they must be specific. Goals that are too general are nothing more than wishes. For example, deciding to improve your communication skills is meaningless unless you also decide exactly what actions you're going to take to make them better, such as determining which courses would be most beneficial to you, which books you're going to buy (and read), and what specific steps you intend to take to increase your vocabulary.

Confused or unclear goals breed apathy and disinterest. People who are trying to reach a definite goal by following a specific plan are far more apt to exert the extra effort required to succeed in reaching their potential. People without definite goals and specific plans don't have the same discipline and incentive, and usually spend more time procrastinating and wondering what they should do next than they spend actually working toward success.

You also have to set a practical timetable for each goal, whether long-term or short-term. Because everyone has to deal with distractions from time to time, goals without timetables are never as effective as those that have them. Getting back to the example of improving your communication skills, you have to decide *when* you're going to enroll in those courses, *when* you're going to buy and read those books, and, for that matter, exactly how and when you intend to add words to your vocabulary. There's no point aiming at something unless you intend to pull the trigger. As Napoleon said, "If you start to take Vienna—take Vienna!"

Ambition is generally a good attribute; you should have to stretch a bit to reach your goals. But if you set your goals unreasonably high, you will become a victim of constant tension and frustration. As mentioned in Chapter 7, it's always expectations that cause frustration, so keep your goals practical and realistic. Aim high enough to stretch yourself but not so high that you give up hope after a try or two. Goals that are difficult but not impossible will keep you moving in the right direction to achieve success and will ultimately provide immense gratification. Unrealistic goals will result in nothing but disappointment.

You need both short-term and long-term goals. You need long-term goals to maintain your momentum, discipline, and inspiration, and to keep you from being frustrated by short-term setbacks. You need short-term goals as effective and measurable stepping stones in achieving your longer-term goals. Achieving short-term goals is also a good confidence builder. Long-term goals, of course, can be set much higher than short-term goals, but even long-term goals should never be set so high that they can't be attained by successfully reaching a series of compatible short-term goals.

The best way to start on the road to a specific long-term goal is to set a reasonable, complementary, and compatible short-term goal. Then when that goal is reached, set another one a little higher. This keeps you going. For example, it would be fine for a professional accountant who has just obtained her designation, and is working for an accounting firm, to set a short-term

goal of getting a promotion to the next employment clas-
sification within a year. It would be totally unrealistic for
her short-term goal to be reaching partnership without
having to go through all the intervening steps, a process
that takes many years. If she doesn't, for whatever reason, get that first promotion as scheduled, it needn't
frustrate the long-term goal of becoming a partner,
because there is still lots of time left to get back on track.

Another reason long-term goals should always be
capable of being broken down into short-term goals is
that reaching long-term goals on a timetable is not
always within your control. When setbacks start to get
you down, set some simpler short-term goals and work
your way back up. Remember, too, that your objectives,
not events, should set your agenda. Suppose that young
accountant takes a maternity leave for a year. She should
not abandon her goal of becoming a partner; she should
simply reset the timetable and adjust the short-term
goals as required.

It's important when setting your goals to remember
that wise people don't waste time and energy on pursuits
for which they are not suited. If you have very limited
musical talent, it might be fine to have as a goal learning
a few chords on the guitar, or how to play a simple tune
on the piano, but it would be ridiculous in the extreme to
make playing in a professional band your goal. The wis-
est people resolutely follow the thing that they do best.
Even if as a superb athlete he could probably do so, why

would Tiger Woods waste time trying to improve his baseball swing? About the only reason I can think of is if he wanted to do it as a simple diversion; he certainly shouldn't do it as part of his golfing regime.

If you're having trouble developing a framework for your goal-setting, try planning ninety-day segments over a three-year period. Ask yourself what has to happen over the next three years to prevent you from looking back and saying, "I wish I had . . . ," or "I wish I hadn't . . ." It might help to think back over the past year or two, identifying your successes and setbacks. Pretend it's three years from now and you've been able to turn time back to today. What would you change? Consider health, free time, career, earnings, financial cushion, and relationships (some people have too many; others not enough). In the meantime, pretend you're going to have a press conference ninety days from now to discuss your activities up to that point. Think about what you'd want to say to the reporters and then plan and act accordingly.

Goals based on quality are always better than goals based on quantity. Let's get back to the goal of increasing your vocabulary. Although you could set your goal to be learning, say, ten new words a week, you're more apt to be successful if your goal is to learn the meaning, spelling, and at least one synonym of each new word that you come across, and to use that new word in a sentence as soon as possible. There are two problems with the numerical goal of ten words a week. The first is that the goal may be set too high, requiring a fixed discipline that's too easily abandoned. The second problem is that the meanings of those words are not likely to be retained, because you will probably be learning words that you won't use. Increasing your vocabulary is far more likely to happen if your short-term approach is to master every new word you come across in your everyday routine. That way, you'll be encountering new words relevant to your daily activities, which will make them more useful and easier to retain. Add the proviso that if you don't come across at least one new word in a particular week, you should grab the dictionary and add one at random. If you don't already own a good dictionary and thesaurus, you should buy them right away. Then, of course, you have to use them.

Finally, don't hesitate to reward yourself in some small way each time you make a significant advance toward reaching a long-term goal. Some people build in their rewards, such as planning a few days' vacation after completing a particular phase of their larger undertaking. Other rewards can be less dramatic, possibly a nice dinner accompanied by a bottle of good wine, or perhaps just taking a short break from your quest. The important point is not the nature of the rewards; it's the positive effect of having them.

REMEMBER:

1. If you don't have a plan of your own, then your only hope is to be part of someone else's.
2. Goals that aren't specific are just wishes.
3. Goals must have practical timetables.
4. Goals must be realistic; unrealistic expectations just cause frustration.
5. You need both long-term and short-term goals.
6. You should always be able to break down your long-term goals into short-term steps.
7. Goals based on quality are better than goals based on quantity.

TO-DO LIST:

1. When setbacks start to get you down, set some simpler short-term goals and work your way back up.
2. Let your objectives, not events, set your agenda.
3. Don't waste time and energy on pursuits for which you are not suited.
4. Reward yourself each time you make a significant advance toward reaching a long-term goal.

EVOLUTION
IS PREFERABLE
TO REVOLUTION

A few years ago a memorable advertising campaign depicted men sporting black eyes and wearing crisp white shirts. The ads said that these men would "rather fight than switch" their brand of cigarettes. The ads were effective because that's the way it is in real life: getting people to change the way they do anything is much like asking them to switch their favourite item of clothing for something that you've chosen for them. Although you're not apt to end up in a fist fight, any time you try to introduce change into people's lives you can usually expect some degree of resistance; quite often you will encounter a great deal of resistance. It's at this point that you have to remind yourself that evolution is preferable to revolution.

Consider for a moment how difficult it is to change your own opinions or way of doing things, and you'll better understand why it is so hard to get others to do so. Yet we often find ourselves in circumstances in which it is necessary to effect changes in the way people think, in the way they do things, or in what they actually do. When you find yourself having to introduce change into people's lives, you will quickly discover that most folks are more comfortable with old problems than they are with new solutions.

Because most people feel threatened to at least some degree by change, there is rarely any surefire way to make them like it. Usually the best you can hope to accomplish is to help them feel less threatened. One way to do this is to clearly demonstrate the advantages that may flow from the change, especially any way in which they will be better off as a result, either as individuals or as a group. In fact, if you can't clearly demonstrate the advantage of the change you want made, you should reconsider whether the change should even be suggested.

People are also less likely to strenuously resist change if they know exactly what lies ahead, and what the recognizable value is of each step along the way. So before you introduce a major change in what people do or how they do it, be sure you've worked out how to clearly communicate such details to everyone who is affected. Another thing to keep in mind is that big changes are usually better understood, and therefore more readily accepted, when presented in bite-size pieces.

When introducing change to a group of people, you must remember that groups are rarely homogeneous. Any group will probably be made up of individuals who have different motivations for being involved, so they won't all be moved by the same arguments and persuasions. You get people to do what you want them to do by understanding what motivates them, not by threatening, bullying, or tricking them. You need to find out what's important to the people affected so that you can craft the change in a way that meets as many of their needs as possible.

People who don't care about a problem won't care about its solution. So always begin by clearly explaining, in terms that are easily understood, the nature of the problem the proposed change is intended to fix and the negative effects it's having, or is going to have, on the people involved if changes aren't made.

The people who do a job are usually the most knowledgeable about it and are the best source of ideas for improving how it is done, so you should start with them when dealing with workplace change. Wise managers always consult their people about any prospective changes, asking for ideas and assistance. Ideas are like children: a person's own are special. By incorporating the views of those who will be most affected by the change, you will make them feel that at least part of the decision was theirs. As a result they will be more inclined to co-operate.

Anytime you're trying to change the status quo, remember that somebody is responsible for it, and it might be the person you're talking to. So try not to be too negative about the current state of things. Concentrate instead on the advantages of the proposed change.

A common mistake made when managing change that involves a large number of people is putting off executing the change while trying to convince everyone of its merits. As much as it would be nice to get everybody onside, trying to do so is usually futile. Don't waste too much time working on the ten percent who will never, under any circumstances, accept the changes you're trying to introduce. Concentrate instead on the ninety percent who can be convinced it's a good idea.

Change in response to success is a lot easier to effect than change in response to failure, so don't wait until something goes drastically wrong before introducing your changes. The ideal scenario would be to plan changes well in advance of the time they need to be implemented, and to introduce them gradually while things are still going well.

You can't usually improve everything all at once, but often a little change now can pave the way for a great change later on. It's very much like the suggestion in the previous chapter that long-term goals are more readily achieved when broken down into a series of short-term goals. For example, when personal computers first became readily available and affordable for most businesses, the organizations that experienced the least resistance to their introduction were the ones that introduced them gradually, starting with the departments where their benefits to the individuals using them would be most obvious. In the organizations that took this approach, employees in the departments that didn't yet have their computers were actually looking forward to the change, whereas the organizations that waited too long, and tried to introduce computers to all their staff at once, usually experienced a great deal of resistance and, in some cases, utter chaos.

The adage that cautions "if it ain't broke, don't fix it" is a good one. In your haste to deal with things that *might* go wrong, be sure you don't tamper with things that are perfectly fine as they are. Old ways might be old for a very good reason—they're actually the best way to do things. Just because something is different doesn't automatically mean that it's better. On the other hand, to begin something new you sometimes have to end something old, even if it's still working fine; replacing typewriters with word processors comes to mind as an example.

When you are the person on the receiving end of a proposed new way of doing something, instead of thinking about all the reasons why it might not work, look for one good reason why it might. In changing circumstances, the phrase "survival of the fittest" should itself be changed to "survival of the most adaptable."

Here are two more thoughts on managing change: First, the world needs smart young people with the imagination and the drive to want to turn everything upside down, but the world also needs old fogies to keep the young from turning upside down things that should remain right side up. And second, most changes are accomplished by compromise; a "my way or the highway" approach is rarely the best way to efficiently effect change.

REMEMBER:

1. Even if you can't make people like change, you can usually find a way to make them feel less threatened by it.

2. People are less likely to resist change when they know exactly what the advantages are, especially any way in which they will be better off, either as individuals or as a group.

3. You get people to do what you want them to do by understanding them, not by bullying, threatening, or tricking them.

4. If people don't care about a problem, they won't care about its solution.

5. People who do a job are usually the best source of ideas for improving how it should be done.

6. Ideas are like children: people's own are special. So involve the people affected when planning changes.

7. Change in response to success is usually more palatable than change in response to failure.

8. Sometimes a little change now can pave the way for a large change later on.

9. Old ways might be old for a very good reason.
10. We need bright, brave young people who want to turn things upside down, but we also need old fogies who know what should remain right side up.
11. Most changes are accomplished by compromise.

TO-DO LIST:

1. Consider how difficult it is to change yourself, and you'll better understand how hard it is to change others.
2. When trying to change the status quo, remember that somebody is responsible for creating it, and it might be the person you're talking to.
3. Don't waste too much time working on the ten percent of the people who will never accept the change.
4. When you are on the receiving end of a proposed change, instead of looking for reasons why it might not work, look for one good reason why it might. In changing circumstances, the phrase "survival of the fittest" should itself be changed to "survival of the most adaptable."

TRUTH IS LIKE SURGERY

People from every walk of life, including a long list of politicians and other public figures, have learned to their dismay that cover-ups are usually more damaging than the original transgressions. It's always difficult to talk your way out of something that you behaved yourself into, so don't even try. When caught out, tell the truth: walk in, plant your feet firmly, look the other person in the eye, and tell it like it is.

Truth is like surgery; it hurts at the time, but it cures in the long run. Lies sometimes seem to get you briefly out of a tight spot, but time and time again they have proven to have no future. If you lie, the odds are overwhelming that you will be found out. The people you've lied to are not going to like it, and could very well be even angrier than they would have been learning of the original blunder. In addition, the stress of carrying the burden of a serious lie will negatively affect your peace of mind and might even eventually affect your physical well-being.

Truth and honesty are necessary for any society to survive. If you're unfailingly honest, at the very least you will know that there is one less deceiver in the world. Truth is never to be feared. In the long run even an embarrassing truth is better for all concerned than a smooth lie.

Half-truths can also be hazardous; there's always the danger that you may pick the wrong half. For example, don't fall into the trap of telling people only what they *want* to hear; tell them what they *ought* to hear (gently and diplomatically, of course). By telling them what they ought to hear, you may save them from making wrong decisions or taking inappropriate actions. In the long run they will also respect you more.

While I was still in grade school, I was first exposed to a very practical reason to avoid lying. I was in class when, for the second time that week, one of my friends gave our teacher an obviously fabricated and very convoluted excuse for not having done his homework. This second excuse also contradicted the equally convoluted one he had given earlier. I was at his house the following Saturday when our teacher arrived to talk to his parents (an event that wasn't extraordinary in the small village where we lived). I went outside to wait, and when my friend joined me later it was obvious that he had been severely busted. But his logic was, and still is, unassailable. "You know," he said, "if I'm going to be telling lies, I'm going to have to start writing them down." Most of us simply don't have good enough memories to count on lies to get us out of trouble. In the total time spent dealing with the fallout from his lies my friend could have done his homework. Truth, it seems, is usually shorter than fiction.

Another lesson, this one learned early in my career, is that it's far better to fail with honour than to succeed by fraud. The company where I was working often had what were referred to as "competitions" for certain jobs. These competitions consisted of written tests that were part aptitude and part technical knowledge. One night there were a number of us working late, two of whom were going to be writing the test for a particular posting in a couple of days. Someone noticed that our supervisor, who had gone home earlier, had left a copy of the test on his desk, and he pointed this out to the two aspiring applicants. One of the two refused to look at it, but the other studied it carefully. Predictably, the chap who studied the test scored very well and got the job. However, he didn't keep it very long. Not only did it quickly become obvious that he wasn't really qualified to hold the position, but the gap between how he did on the test and how he performed on the job was so great that his unauthorized preview of the test was eventually discovered and he was fired.

In addition to being brutally honest yourself, you should be wary of anyone who is willing to be dishonest on your behalf. I never again completely trusted the employee who pointed out that the test was on the supervisor's desk. It's likely that anyone who would cheat for you would cheat on you.

REMEMBER:

1. Cover-ups usually cause more problems than the original mistakes.
2. It's hard to talk your way out of something that you behaved yourself into.
3. The trouble with a half-truth is that you might have the wrong half.
4. The burden of a serious lie will negatively affect your peace of mind and possibly your physical health.
5. Few people have good enough memories to be consistently successful liars.
6. Anyone who would cheat for you will probably cheat on you.

TO-DO LIST:

1. When in doubt, always tell the truth.
2. Be unfailingly honest and you will know for sure that there is one less deceiver in the world.
3. Fail with honour rather than succeed by fraud.
4. Don't allow anyone to be dishonest on your behalf.

CHARACTER TRUMPS REPUTATION

Many people think that their level of success is defined by their reputation. The truth is that your character is going to be much more important in defining your success than your reputation ever will be. Character defines the person you really are, regardless of the circumstances in which you find yourself. Your reputation, on the other hand, is only what some people think you are in certain circumstances.

Be more concerned about your character than you are about your reputation, and your reputation will take care of itself. In the long term, your reputation will become a by-product of your character. If you are of strong character, your consistent exemplary behaviour will mean that even insulting remarks about you will be meaningless because nobody will believe them.

Your character isn't going to be judged by what you *say* you believe in, or what you *say* about how people should act; your character will be judged by how you actually live your life. This is another lesson that I was fortunate to learn first-hand.

I was working with a gentleman named Brian Williams, a very common name but a very uncommon man. One winter day, just after a snowstorm, he was driving to a sporting event in a fairly isolated suburb of Toronto. Brian was a relatively new driver with a relatively old car. He was inching his way along an icy patch when he lost control and skidded into the side of a parked vehicle. Brian's bumper took the impact, with the result that there was no damage at all to his car, but the door on the driver's side of the other car was badly dented. The vehicle he hit was the only one on the road, and it was obvious from the amount of snow on it that it had been parked there for some time. There wasn't a person in sight and there were no houses close enough for anyone to be able to clearly see Brian's licence number. But Brian left a note with his name and telephone number on it. *That's* character.

It's always a good measure of character to observe how people behave when they think no one is watching. People with character don't change their ethics according to circumstances. Those who would have left a note on the damaged car if they thought someone might have gotten their licence number, but wouldn't have under Brian's circumstances, are not in the same character league as Brian.

A person of strong character, upon realizing she is wrong, quickly admits it. The most successful people that I've had the pleasure of working with never had a problem admitting they were wrong, a characteristic that not only saved a lot of time but also enhanced their reputations.

The respect earned by displays of good character is much easier kept than recovered. It's obvious that I formed a very high opinion of Brian's character on that wintry day. But suppose he had gotten out, put a blank sheet of paper under the other car's windshield wiper, and then said, "Anyone watching will think I left my name and number." How many future demonstrations of ethical behaviour on Brian's part do you think it would have taken for me to reach the same level of respect for his character as I did from learning what he'd actually done? I seriously doubt that he could ever have recovered my respect.

It's often been said that playing a sport builds character. This may be true in some small respect when children play team sports during those formative years. But, based on my extensive experience in dealing with athletes, when it comes to adults it's more accurate to say that playing a sport *reveals* character. Temptation, adversity, greed, fear, and power all test and reveal character; all are present in sport and all are present in everyday life. How you act in these situations will reveal your true character.

The following ten rules will help you be true to yourself when you find your character being severely tested.

- If you're going to insist on having your rights, be prepared to live up to your responsibilities.
- The right motive is more important than the right move; do things because they're right, not because they're clever.
- Don't let others set your standards; be true to yourself.
- To be trusted, be trustworthy.
- Toughness is a means, not an end.
- Moral courage is rarer than physical bravery; what's often mistaken for bravery is often just bad judgment.
- When you're faced with moral decisions, remember that it's really your character that's being tested, not your reputation.
- To live a worthwhile life, decide what you want written on your tombstone.
- A good reputation may be a wonderful way to open doors, but only character will keep them open. Phonies and con men are soon found out— and then usually ushered out.
- It's never too late to become the person you want to be.

REMEMBER:

1. Your character will be judged by how you actually live your life.
2. Insulting remarks about you will never harm

your reputation if you live so that nobody will
believe them.

3. A good reputation gained through character is
much easier kept than recovered.

TO-DO LIST:

1. Be more concerned about your character than
about your reputation.

2. Don't change your ethics according to
circumstances.

3. When you find your character being severely
tested, remember the ten rules for being true to
yourself.

COMMUNICATE WELL AND
DO WELL, COMMUNICATE BEST
AND FLOURISH

Chapter 1 outlined the importance of developing and honing the skills needed to achieve success in whatever endeavours you undertake. By far the most important skill in assuring long-lasting success in most endeavours is the ability to communicate well.

Whatever you are—a student, a clerk, a receptionist, an intern, an executive, an entrepreneur, a professional, a politician, a fundraiser, or simply a concerned citizen who wants to make a difference in your community—you will not reach your true potential unless you acquire the necessary communication skills.

Competent, well-educated, talented people often find their earning capacities limited because they can't adequately communicate their ideas. As unfair as it may seem, poor eye contact and mumbling have been known to completely sidetrack careers. Poorly written documents can seriously delay an employee's progress through the ranks.

Your ability to communicate will determine whether

you're memorable or forgettable, boring or interesting, and whether you will be able to influence people or simply be ignored. The inability to organize and clearly articulate ideas has prevented people from all walks of life from achieving their goals and reaching their potential. If you can't write and speak effectively, you are at a tremendous disadvantage.

Just think about it in these terms: There is no point in knowing how to solve a problem if you can't communicate the solution in a way that people will understand and that will persuade them to act. But it's been proven time and time again that if you have something worthwhile to say, and you know how to say it well, the whole world will listen.

People are influenced by articulate, well-organized, effective communicators. Whatever it is you set out to do, if you communicate well, you will do well, but if you communicate best, you will flourish.

In our current environment, business leaders and professionals can no longer succeed by maintaining a low profile. Just as politicians and celebrities have been for years, business leaders and professionals are now wide open to public and private scrutiny, and to succeed they must have the ability to communicate well to people both within and outside their organizations.

It isn't just business leaders and professionals who need to hone their communication skills. Concerned citizens wishing to make a difference in their communities must develop the same communication skills as do business executives and professionals. Taking the time to write an effective letter or to prepare and deliver an effective presentation may convince your local council to install those speed bumps that could save lives. Maybe you simply want to appropriately welcome your new son-in-law into the family, or pay a fitting tribute to a deserving teacher who is retiring. Whatever the occasion and whatever your objective, an effective presentation will enhance both your chances of achieving the result you want and your reputation as a leader.

This all may sound very daunting, but there is really good news. The ability to communicate effectively is not an art that you need to be born with; it is a skill that can be learned, just like swimming or riding a bicycle.

There's even more good news. Teaching public speaking for over forty years has convinced me that nothing builds a person's overall self-confidence as much as acquiring the ability to be an effective public speaker. Once you become an effective public speaker, the resulting self-confidence will spill over into all aspects of your life, and you will become a more successful and effective person in everything that you do. Enhancing your writing skills comes a close second in building this kind of self-confidence.

To be a fully rounded communicator, you need to develop your skills in a number of areas. In addition to developing conversation and listening skills, you need to develop skills in the areas of writing, public speaking, and, in some instances, dealing with the media. The next five chapters each deal with one of these five communication challenges.

REMEMBER:

1. The inability to communicate well has prevented people from all walks of life from achieving their goals and reaching their potential.

2. People are influenced by articulate, well-organized, effective communicators.

3. There's no point knowing the solution to a problem if you can't communicate that solution in a way that people will understand and will then persuade them to act.

4. If you have something worthwhile to say, and you know how to say it well, the whole world will listen.

5. In any situation, being able to communicate well will enhance both your chances of success and your reputation as a leader.

6. The ability to communicate effectively is a skill, not an art; it can be learned.

7. Nothing builds overall self-confidence as much as becoming an effective public speaker. Becoming an effective writer is a close second.

TO-DO LIST:

1. Develop your conversation, listening, writing, and presentation skills.
2. If you're going to be dealing with the media, be sure to review Chapter 18.

WHEN ALL ELSE FAILS, ASK ABOUT THE DOG

The ability to effectively carry on a conversation, whether with a stranger, colleague, or friend, is an important element of success for a variety of reasons. There is no doubt that being a good conversationalist will enhance your reputation as a communicator. Furthermore, people enjoy being in the company of a good conversationalist, so it will create opportunities to expand your network of contacts. Being a good conversationalist will also make you a popular neighbour and a sought-after dinner guest. Last, and certainly not least, you will learn things.

Although some people seem to be born with the "gift of the gab," most good conversationalists have had to learn and refine their conversation skills. Like anything worthwhile, until it becomes second nature to you, being a good conversationalist requires work.

Make sure that your conversation isn't just a monologue delivered to an unwitting captive audience. No one likes being around a long-winded motormouth who never lets other people speak. A sure warning that you might be talking more than your share is if you frequently catch yourself saying "to make a long story short." Most people don't make a long story short until it is already too late. A good rule of thumb is to always say less than you know about any subject.

Another potential conversational problem to watch for is what's usually referred to as a slip of the tongue, the unintentional oral faux pas that tends to get people in trouble. As some wit once put it, probably right after saying something regrettable, "the tongue, being wet, is prone to slip." This most often happens when you're in a conversation with people whom you don't know well. Until you get to know a little bit about people you've just met, be very circumspect about your comments. It's usually wise to stay away from intense discussions about religion or politics.

Clever remarks can also cause problems in conversations with people whom you don't know well. Actually, overly clever remarks can even get you in trouble with your friends. Always take the time to consider how biting your clever remark is, and whether you should even say it. A clever retort should always be sacrificed for the sake of someone's feelings. Remember that real wit (a rare and usually appreciated skill) should be the seasoning of a conversation; it should never be the main course. Wiseacres are never appreciated and are rarely tolerated for long.

Just as motormouths and wiseacres are never on the list of good conversationalists, another common undesirable at the water cooler, cocktail party, or dinner table is the know-it-all. It's always better to ask some of the questions than to pretend to know all of the answers; indeed, it's often a good idea to pretend to learn things that you already know. In some situations, all you have to do to be considered a good conversationalist is to be a good listener. Listening skills, an integral requirement for being a good conversationalist, are sufficiently important to be the focus of the next chapter.

Some people do just fine once a conversation gets going but find it difficult to initiate one. Asking a question is the most effective technique for starting a conversation, even if it's only, "Have you ever seen such lousy weather?"

Asking questions is also the best way to keep a conversation going; it keeps the discussion balanced and enjoyable for all concerned, so take advantage of any opportunity to ask a question rather than make a statement. For example, it's a lot more effective to ask, "Why are you going to support that candidate?" rather than saying, "I don't understand why you would vote for that jerk."

The best questions in any conversation start with words that begin with a *w*, such as: "Why do you say that?"; "Where are you going to be staying?"; "What would have to happen in order for you to change your mind?"; "When did all this happen?"; "Who else is going to be involved?" The second-best questions start with words that begin with the letter *h*, such as: "Have you thought about . . . ?"; "Had you expected . . . ?"; "How do you intend to raise the money?" However, a few words of caution are in order here. A good conversationalist asks the questions that people want to answer, not ones that make them uncomfortable. Furthermore, you're not going to carry on an effective conversation if you continually sound like you're interrogating or cross-examining everyone. In addition to asking questions, you also need to make your own contributions to a conversation.

In conversation, how you say something may determine the nature and substance of the response. Always ask questions and make statements in a friendly tone of voice. Remember, we're talking about conversations here, not debates. However, if the discussion should take a turn for the worse, it's always worth the effort to keep your tone of voice on an even keel. Consider hostile questions as simply requests for information, and when someone complains to you about something, assume at the outset that the complaint is legitimate. There's no need to raise your voice if the right words are used; it's a lot easier to eat angry words now than it will be to have them forced down your throat later.

You should always be as ready to accept other people's ideas as you are your own, keeping in mind that one difference between a conviction and a prejudice is that a conviction can be explained without raising your voice. Most of the friction of daily living is caused by the wrong tone of voice. Granted, it sometimes takes a lot of discipline to keep your tone of voice on an even keel, but it's always worth the effort.

If you're like most people, you'll find there are times when your mind wanders or you just lose interest in the conversation. For any number of reasons, your mind can go momentarily blank during a conversation. So, when you realize you've lost the signal, be sure to turn off the sound. And then be sure you pick up the thread of the conversation again before jumping in and making some regrettable comment. An ounce of "don't say it" is worth a ton of "I didn't mean it."

One of the suggestions in Dale Carnegie's famous book *How to Win Friends and Influence People* is to become genuinely interested in other people. This certainly holds true for becoming a good conversationalist. People like to talk about what's important to them, and what's important to them is whatever they think is important, regardless of how unimportant it may seem to you. Remember, too, that the deepest human craving is for appreciation, so sincere praise will always be more effective in enhancing your reputation as a conversationalist than criticism. As a matter of fact, saying nothing of consequence is usually more effective in a social conversation than criticizing someone.

Although you don't want to carry this approach to the point where people will think you have no ideas, convictions, or interesting experiences of your own, to the extent it's possible, talk about the things other people want to talk about rather than talking about yourself. As someone once put it, there's no need to talk too much about yourself; others will do that when you leave the room.

Even if you adhere religiously to all of the above rules and read Dale Carnegie's book every three months, you're still not going to be completely happy with the way all your conversations go. There are bound to be times when you may be saying all the right things but the other person, for whatever reason, simply isn't ready to hear them. You can't always get into other people's minds, so don't become disheartened when your best efforts fall short. Remember what I said in Chapter 2 about a person's prevalent train of thought. The other person's toothache is, to them, far more important than your wonderful cruise, and if they're wrestling with a particularly worrisome problem, they may be too preoccupied to chat at all.

When all else fails, ask about the dog.

REMEMBER:

1. Wit should be the seasoning of a conversation, never the main course.
2. The best questions in any conversation start with words that begin with *w*.

3. The second-best questions start with words that begin with *h*.

4. A good conversationalist asks the questions people want to answer.

5. One difference between a conviction and a prejudice is that a conviction can be explained without raising your voice.

6. How you say something may determine another person's response to it; most of the friction of daily living is caused by the wrong tone of voice. There's no need to shout if the right words are used.

7. It's always easier to swallow angry words now than to have them shoved down your throat later.

8. What's important to people is whatever they think is important.

9. There's no need to talk too much about yourself; others will do that when you leave the room.

10. You may be saying all the right things but the other person may, for whatever reason, simply not be ready to hear them.

TO-DO LIST:

1. Make sure your conversation isn't just a monologue delivered in front of a captive audience.

2. Make your long story short before it's too late to do so.

3. When in conversation with people you don't know well, avoid slips of the tongue. Especially avoid discussing religion and politics.

4. Ask some of the questions rather than supplying all the answers.

5. Pretend to learn things you already know.

6. Don't make a statement when you can ask a question.

7. Be as ready to accept other people's ideas as you are your own.

8. Consider even hostile questions as simply requests for information.

9. When receiving a complaint, assume at the outset that it's legitimate.

10. Become genuinely interested in other people.

GOOD LISTENERS
AREN'T JUST POPULAR,
THEY LEARN THINGS

Early in my accounting career, if someone came over to my desk to talk to me, I would continue to work on whatever I was doing. I always heard what was being said and I actually thought that I was being very efficient. I learned my first important listening lesson one day when a colleague was telling me about a problem she was having, that she thought I could help her with. I continued to post numbers in a ledger while she explained her situation to me. Suddenly, she shouted, "You're not listening!" I told her I *had* been listening and thought I'd redeemed myself by repeating, almost word for word, everything she had said. She retorted, "But your eyes weren't listening." Of course, she was right; as far as she was concerned I hadn't been listening in any sort of meaningful way.

To be a good listener, you must give the person who is talking to you your full attention. This means, in addition to maintaining eye contact, paying attention to her body language, facial expression, and tone of voice.

Entire books have been written on the interpretation of body language, but you don't have to be an expert to understand the contrast between a person who is fidgeting and bouncing from one foot to the other and someone who is calmly standing straight and gesturing confidently. A pained expression is more revealing than the words "I'm all right." Similarly, a snappish, snarling "I'm just fine, thank you," indicates an emotional condition at odds with the words. If you aren't looking the speaker right in the eye, you'll be creating the same impression I did with my co-worker many years ago. By paying attention to facial expressions, body language, and tone of voice, you will better understand the other person's emotional state, which isn't always accurately conveyed by words alone.

It's equally important to maintain eye contact when you're speaking with someone in a crowd of people. If your eyes are wandering, you are sending a message that you're looking for someone more interesting or more important to talk to, even if that isn't the case.

As mentioned in the previous chapter, in some situations listening is all you have to do to be considered a good conversationalist. One night, as a head-table guest at a business dinner, I was seated at the left end of the table, so I had only the woman on my right to talk to during the course of the evening. She was the after-dinner speaker's wife, and although I knew her husband quite well, I hadn't met her before. Throughout the evening, while she and I were conversing, she probably talked for ninety percent of the time. Yet, when I ran into her husband a few days later, he told me what a wonderful conversationalist his wife thought I was. Basically, all I had done was listen attentively to what she had to say.

The truth is that many people wouldn't listen at all if they didn't think it was their turn next. As a result, these people commit the most egregious listening sin—thinking about what *they're* going to say when it's their turn to speak rather than paying full attention to what is being said to them. Good listening needs your undivided attention. Don't listen just to decide what you're going to say when it's your turn; listen instead to understand *exactly* what the other person is saying. Only then should you think about how you're going to reply. This may take a few extra seconds, but it will never take as much time as having to undo misunderstandings. Paying close attention to what the other person has to say has the added benefit of allowing you to respond in a more focused way, which will make for a more interesting conversation.

Listen for *intent* as well as *content*. When you start to hear fuzzy generalities, especially from a person who is usually very clear in what they're saying, ask a specific question. That way, you're more apt to find out what the other person is really trying to say. Remember, the best way to get clear answers is to ask clear questions. The fuzzier the other person's answers, the clearer your questions must be.

You shouldn't tune out a person simply because there's something about them that you don't like. Listen to everyone; everyone has ideas, and ideas are sometimes more valuable than money. If you and I exchange five-dollar bills, we each still have only five dollars. But if we exchange an idea, we each now have two ideas to think about.

You need to be careful not to overreact to ideas that question your beliefs. In these circumstances it's particularly important to withhold judgment until you hear everything the other person has to say. Don't fall into the trap of tuning out after the first few words of a sentence because you've already decided what the other person is talking about; they may be leaving something quite unexpected until the end.

There are times when it requires an effort for you to speak up, but there are also times when it takes an effort to keep quiet. Applause is the only interruption that's ever appreciated by any speaker, be it in front of an audience of one hundred or an audience of one, so don't interrupt anyone, no matter how strong the temptation might be.

Good listeners aren't just popular; they get to know things. When we're talking, we can only repeat what we know, but when we are listening we learn what other people know.

The other side of listening too little is usually talking too much. If you try to dominate a conversation, you'll never be a popular conversationalist and, perhaps even more important, you won't learn anything.

REMEMBER:

1. Listening is all you need to do to please some people.
2. Good listening needs your undivided attention.
3. The other side of listening too little is talking too much.

TO-DO LIST:

1. Always maintain eye contact with anyone who is speaking to you.
2. Listen carefully to what people say, but don't neglect clues indicating how they feel, such as body language, facial expression, and tone of voice.
3. Don't listen to decide what you're going to say; listen to understand what the other person is actually saying.
4. Listen for *intent* as well as *content*.
5. Don't tune out people simply because you don't like something about them.
6. Don't overreact to ideas that question your beliefs.
7. Don't tune out after the first few words of a sentence, assuming you know the rest of what that person has to say.
8. Don't interrupt.

WHEN YOU THINK YOU'RE
FINISHED, READ IT
ONE MORE TIME

This chapter won't turn you into a best-selling novelist, but if you heed the following advice, your personal and business writing (reports, memos, letters, and emails) will be much more effective.

The first thing to remember about writing anything, from a one-paragraph email to a voluminous report, is that the reader is not going to have the benefit of hearing your tone of voice or your inflection. Nor will the reader be able to see the expression on your face or your body language. And if they become confused, recipients of your communication are not going to be able to stop you and ask for clarification. Accordingly, you have to choose your written words far more carefully than you do your spoken words. The more important the communication, the more attention that needs to be paid to your choice of words, but even the simplest of written communications should be carefully crafted.

Because writing has to be more precise than speech,

you need to choose your words not only so they can be understood but also so that they cannot be misunderstood. This requires additional thought and often takes more time than you would like. But it usually doesn't take as much time and thought as would clearing up misunderstandings later. It's also a lot less dangerous; libel suits have been lost because of imprecise writing.

Use impact words; they're usually more precise than generalities. For example,

Smashed is stronger than *broken*.
Thrilled is more descriptive than *happy*.
Weary is more emphatic than *tired*.
Magnificent is more impressive than *very good*.
Sweltering is a vast improvement on *very warm*.

Whenever you find yourself using the word "very," take the time to find a single, more descriptive word. This is a good time to mention again that you should always have a thesaurus and a dictionary within reach, and you should reach for them often.

To the greatest extent possible, make your communications human rather than institutional. The biggest problem with most business writing is that it is too stuffy and formal. For example,

DON'T SAY:	SAY:
further notification will follow in due course	I'll keep you up to date as things develop
give consideration to	consider
during the course of	during
endeavour	try

Instead of saying, "Appropriate amendments will be introduced in a timely fashion," say, "We'll make changes as soon as the committee considers the matter, which will likely be before the end of the month."

Avoid flowery prose. "A person's desire for possession of material goods will, from time to time, overwhelm one's innate sense of prudence," is a very elegant sentence. However, you have a far better chance of being understood if you say, "Greed often prevails over common sense."

Anytime you catch yourself writing "in other words," the preceding words obviously didn't adequately make your point, so they need to be rewritten. If you don't come up with the words needed to plant clear images in the minds of your readers, they'll come up with their own images. And the images they conjure up may not fit the images you're trying to convey.

There is another very simple way to improve your business writing and set your communications apart from the boring run-of-the-mill institutional standard that seems to be the norm. It's getting rid of trite phrases, expressions that, although meaningful at one time or in a particular context, through overuse have become meaningless generalizations. Trite phrases are the clichés of the business world, and tend to be used by executives and professionals who are either in too much of a rush or just too lazy to search for an accurate, descriptive word or phrase. Trite phrases are always boring. They also cheat the reader out of a clear explanation of the message you're trying to convey.

Examples of trite phrases currently popular with business executives and professionals who are too lazy to search for and develop the specific messages they want to convey include

At the end of the day
Going forward
Best practices
Value added
Ramp up
Tone at the top
Thinking outside the box
Tipping point
In terms of
Ahead of (or behind) the curve

If you tend to use trite phrases, you need to break the habit. Eliminating trite phrases from your communications will make you a much more effective writer.

It's usually more effective to talk about what you are *for* rather than what you're *against*, so whenever you have a choice, be positive rather than negative. Readers tend to relate more favourably to positive messages than sour whining and complaining.

Be specific. Generalizations are dull, boring, and uninformative. "We had 102 emails, 32 telephone calls, and 8 letters" is much better than "We had numerous responses."

The active voice is always more powerful than the passive voice. For example, compare "The dog chased the cat" (active) and "The cat was chased by the dog" (passive). The active voice is not only twenty-eight percent shorter than the passive voice, but it immediately conjures up an image of what's happening. Verbs should be as close to their nouns as possible, and a few short sentences are usually more effective than one long, drawn-out mind-boggler. However, keep in mind that it is important to vary the length of your sentences.

When you use a pronoun, especially third-person pronouns, check to ensure that there's no mistaking its antecedent. Compare "He then told him that either he or I would be happy to meet with either of them" to "David then told Marty that either David or I would be happy to meet with him or Bob." What the latter lacks in grace, it more than makes up in clarity, and would be very unlikely to cause the reader any confusion about who's offering to meet with whom.

Each paragraph should deal with only one topic. As with sentences, paragraphs should vary in length and never be too long. In business communications, any paragraph containing more than ten typewritten lines runs the risk of losing the reader's attention. Conversely, every now and then a one-sentence paragraph can be used effectively for emphasis.

Be sure there's some variety in the opening words of your sentences and paragraphs. Four consecutive sentences or paragraphs beginning with the word "I" will likely be interpreted as pomposity and laziness.

Get to your point right away. Unless you're writing a mystery novel, saving the main idea until the end of your communication will simply lose your readers. No one is going to concentrate through four or five paragraphs before getting to your point.

Be sure that anything not directly related to the main theme of your communication actually contributes to the reader's understanding in some way. Otherwise, leave it out. However, be sure you don't omit points that would enhance your reader's understanding of the main message.

When dealing with more than one topic, ensure that each is developed fully with adequate examples, arguments, reasons, and illustrations before moving on to the next. But don't overload your communications with more evidence than your readers require to fully understand your points. One strong example is better than ten wishy-washy ones.

Move in an orderly, logical way from your opening to your closing. Rambling prose with points presented in a nonlogical order will confuse your readers rather than inform them.

You can never go wrong by using Kipling's "six honest serving men": who, what, where, why, how, and when. In utilizing these interrogatives, you cover all the necessary bases. Then take it one step further by anticipating the skeptical reader's "so what?" and writing accordingly.

Stick to plain language. Avoid jargon and buzzwords unless you're certain that your readers will fully understand their meanings. However, jargon and buzzwords are sometimes useful because they serve as a convenient form of shorthand for cumbersome titles and phrases. For example, CEO and GPS are perfectly acceptable when referring to "chief executive officer" and "global positioning system." If there's a good reason to use jargon or buzzwords, by all means do so; but if there's even a remote possibility that your reader won't know what you're talking about, you must define each term when you first use it.

Any important document or communication needs to be edited. Even a short, simple communication needs to be reread before being sent. If it's a long document, it's best to set it aside for an hour or two before editing. If it's not possible to set it aside for that long, leave it while you fetch a coffee or make a couple of calls before starting to edit. When editing long documents, you have to be especially critical of your opening and your closing, the opening because at that point you probably hadn't warmed up, and the closing because by then you may have become tired and less vigilant. Anything you write while tired, angry, or bored needs to be thoroughly edited. It's always a mistake to send off a communication written in anger without setting it aside until you cool off. It might also be a good idea to get a reaction from your executive assistant or another trusted colleague.

Double-check all names, numbers, and quotations. And when you think you're finished, read it one more time.

REMEMBER:

1. Because your reader can't hear your voice, see your facial expressions and body language, or ask you questions, you have to be far more exacting when choosing written words than spoken words.

2. The time and effort required to find and use precise words are usually less than what would be required later to clear up misunderstandings.

3. If you think you need to write "in other words," you need to rewrite what came before.

4. When there's a choice, it's better to be positive rather than negative.

5. The active voice is always more powerful and effective than the passive voice.

6. There should be no doubt as to the antecedent of a pronoun.

7. Verbs should be as close to their nouns as possible.

8. Sentence and paragraph length should vary, but never let them get too long.

9. Anything written while you were tired, angry, or bored needs to be thoroughly edited.

TO-DO LIST:

1. Use impact words rather than generalizations.

2. As much as possible, make your communications human rather than institutional.

3. Eliminate trite phrases from your writing.

4. Rather than use the word "very," take the time to find a single, more descriptive word.

5. Always have a thesaurus and dictionary within easy reach, and reach often.

6. Be specific. Generalizations are dull, boring, and uninformative.

7. Be sure there's variety in the opening words of your sentences and paragraphs.

8. Get to your point quickly.

9. Omit anything that doesn't add to the main

theme, but don't omit anything that would enhance the understanding of your message.

10. Ensure that each topic is fully developed with necessary examples, arguments, reasons, and illustrations, but never more than the reader needs in order to understand your points.

11. Don't ramble; keep your messages moving in a logical manner from beginning to end.

12. Don't just answer who, what, where, why, how, and when; also answer, "so what?"

13. Unless your readers will understand buzzwords or jargon, either replace them or define them.

14. Always edit your document; if it's a long document, preferably after having set it aside for a time.

15. Double-check all names, numbers, and quotations.

KNOW WHAT YOU'RE TALKING ABOUT

Many people feel that making a presentation to colleagues, fellow club members, or a committee meeting is not really public speaking, and fail to approach such occasions as seriously as if they were speaking to a large "outside" audience. As a result they don't prepare properly, seldom if ever rehearse their presentation, and forget that the same basic skills are required whether they're speaking to an audience of friends or strangers, to five people or to five hundred.

The most critical aspect of any presentation you make is that you be speaking on the right topic. Fortunately, there is an extremely useful formula for determining the right topic for you. The formula is so effective that if your topic meets all three of its criteria, a successful presentation is guaranteed. The criteria are

- you must have significant knowledge about the topic;
- you must feel strongly about the topic;

- you must be eager to share your knowledge and feelings with the audience you're going to be addressing.

Dale Carnegie, the undisputed patron saint of public speaking, began using this approach to identifying an appropriate topic almost a century ago. The way he put it was that you have to have earned the right to talk about your topic, you have to be excited about it, and you have to want to talk about it.

If you have significant knowledge about your topic, you'll be able to recover your place after distractions, interruptions, or losing your train of thought, and you'll have the confidence to keep speaking effectively. If you feel strongly about your topic, you'll be too busy concentrating on your message to fall into the trap of worrying about how you look and sound. If you're eagerly looking forward to addressing an audience, you'll deliver your talk with such feeling and enthusiasm that your audience will catch your mood. The formula is so effective, if you meet all the criteria, you probably couldn't fail even if you tried.

You can certainly be forgiven if you think this is an overly optimistic promise, but it is not. As a public speaking coach I've critiqued thousands of speeches, and I've sat in the audience for hundreds more presentations. I can say without reservation that I've *never* seen a speaker fail when all three criteria have been met.

The other side of this coin, of course, is that if you try to make a speech about a topic that you don't know well, you *will* fail. It's not possible to have a successful speaking experience when you don't know enough about your subject. A competent public speaking coach *might* be able to guide you through a lack of desire to talk about a topic, but the best speaking coach in the world can't save you if you don't know what you're talking about.

There are two ways to gain enough knowledge about a topic to be sure that you can address it: study and experience. Having *both* study and experience to support what you're about to say will give you confidence when you speak, and confidence that you're qualified to make this presentation. As a rule of thumb, if you know more about the topic than most of the people in the audience, it's an appropriate topic for you to speak about to that particular group. Never be concerned that there may be one or two people in the audience who know more about the topic than you do. They will still be interested in hearing about your experiences and finding out what you have to say. Otherwise, they wouldn't be there.

When you know you have the right topic, the next step is to prepare.

In order to properly prepare a presentation, you need to find out as much as you can about your audience. This is not a problem when you're addressing colleagues and associates, but if it's an audience that you don't know much about, you need to make some inquiries about the backgrounds of the people likely to attend, their level of knowledge about the subject, and what their expectations are. You can never have too much knowledge about your audience. The more you know about your audience, the easier it will be for you to craft a presentation that will provide them with the information they're coming to hear.

Another reason to find out as much as you can about your audience is because, although it's rare, you may discover that some or all of them might be antagonistic. They might be mildly antagonistic about something as simple as mandatory attendance at your presentation, or they might be very antagonistic, for example, if your objective is to describe an unpopular operating change to a group of recalcitrant employees. In these circumstances, it's important to find some common ground with the audience. Find at least one objective that you share with them, develop some points on which they can agree, and introduce these at the beginning of your presentation.

When facing any audience, especially an antagonistic one, there's always the chance that you will encounter a heckler. You will rarely come out ahead by getting into a mudslinging match. The rest of the audience will usually be on your side at the outset of the heckling, but if you argue with the heckler, your support will start to disappear. Be firm and courteous, but keep control of the situation. Being diplomatic will count for more than being clever, so maintain your composure. An effective technique is to suggest to the heckler that you'll be happy to discuss the issue one-on-one after your presentation; then ignore him. If this doesn't work you may have to resort to asking whoever is in charge to have the heckler cautioned or, in extreme circumstances, removed.

Even if you're going to be speaking from notes rather than a script, you should always write out your speech in full. There are five good reasons to do this.

- It's the best way to develop a consistent message and style.
- You can check the length of your speech by timing how long it takes you to read it out loud, using appropriate pacing and emphasis. (Of course, the best way to check its length is by rehearsing with a stopwatch.)
- It's easier to organize and edit your remarks.
- It helps you decide whether, and where in the presentation, to use visual aids.
- It helps you develop the level of familiarity with your material that you need to be completely comfortable at the lectern.

Use simple, direct language and speak in a conversational tone. Language that is anything other than simple and conversational will get in the way of your message and is more apt to confuse your audience than it is to inform and persuade them. Your audience is not going to be able to consult a dictionary while you're speaking, and if they don't know what you mean they're not going to be persuaded by what you say. Speak exactly the way you would in an animated discussion among friends or at the dinner table.

Unless in a teaching situation or introducing a new concept to the audience, use visual aids sparingly and carefully. You wouldn't want to compete with another event while you are speaking, and overly produced visual aids (especially sound and light shows) will compete with you for your audience's attention.

It's hard to understand why people who would never expect to play like Oscar Peterson the first time they sit down at a piano think they should be able to speak as well as Winston Churchill without a great deal of practice and rehearsing. Even seasoned presenters have to rehearse their presentations in order to perform at their best. So will you.

Provided the expectations of the audience are met, there's no such thing as a speech that's too short. Lincoln's Gettysburg Address was only 268 words long. A good rule of thumb is to prepare material for about eighty percent of your allotted time. This will ensure that you don't run overtime, provide for possible interruptions, and allow you to use any new thoughts that come to mind as you're giving your speech.

This chapter contains the most important points to remember when preparing and making a presentation. No matter how many presentations you've made, you will still benefit from getting some presentation skills training. You should also buy a good book on public speaking and consult it before every presentation you give.

As mentioned in Chapter 13, you'll enjoy a very important bonus from enhancing your presentation skills and becoming comfortable speaking in front of groups. The confidence you gain from the practice and experience of public speaking will overlap all aspects of your life.

REMEMBER:

1. The same public speaking rules apply whether you're making a presentation to friends or strangers, to five people or to five hundred.

2. You must be speaking on the right topic for you.

3. As Dale Carnegie said, you must earn the right to talk about your topic, be excited about it, and want to talk about it.

4. It's not possible to have a successful speaking experience when you don't know what you're talking about.

5. You get to know what you're talking about through study and experience; a topic based on both study and experience is obviously right for you.

6. A good rule of thumb: if you know more about

the topic than most of the people in the audience, it's clearly an appropriate subject.

7. Write out your speech, even if you're going to be speaking from notes.

8. All speakers, even seasoned ones, need to rehearse their presentations.

9. Provided you meet the expectations of the audience, there's no such thing as a speech that's too short.

10. Gaining public speaking skills significantly enhances your overall self-confidence.

TO-DO LIST:

1. Never be concerned that there might be one or two people in the audience who may know more about your topic than you do. They will still be interested in hearing your opinions and finding out about your experiences.

2. If you don't already know enough about your audience, find out as much as you can about them before you prepare your presentation.

3. Use simple, direct language.

4. Speak in a conversational tone, just as you would in an animated discussion among friends or at the dinner table.

5. Except in teaching situations or when introducing a new concept to an audience, use visual aids sparingly and carefully.

6. Take some formal public speaking training.
7. Buy a good book on public speaking and consult it before every presentation.

THE JOURNALIST HAS NOTHING TO LOSE, BUT YOU MIGHT

Most of you will never have to deal with the media. For many more of you, dealing with the media will be a once-in-a-lifetime experience, such as when there's a newsworthy event in your neighbourhood. But some of you, through your professional or volunteer activities, will have more frequent occasion to deal with the media, and when you do, there are some important principles to keep in mind. I mentioned in Chapter 2 that two ways by which people judge you are what you say and how you say it. This is particularly so when you are dealing with the media. (I need to point out here that the advice contained in this chapter is directed to people who are dealing with the media for the first time, not people who regularly appear on radio and television and in print. Those folks have access to professionals who help them determine what to say and how to say it.)

Possibly the most important point to remember when dealing with the media is to be yourself. Whether you're dealing with radio, television, or print journalists, don't try to be somebody you're not; just be yourself, warts and all.

When dealing with the media, you have to be a conscientious listener. You must give your undivided attention to what the journalist is asking. Don't start formulating your answer until you've heard the journalist's entire question, otherwise you may not understand exactly what the question is about. Furthermore, the journalist could throw in an unexpected twist at the very end of the question. Overlooking that subtlety when you answer the question could be embarrassing.

You also have to remember which hat you're wearing. Questions don't always have a crystal-clear context, but answers will always have at least a perceived context. For example, you would have far more credibility discussing the dreadful condition of the town's streets when speaking as the president of the chamber of commerce than you would if you're speaking as the president of a street-paving firm. In circumstances where even a perceived conflict of interest is possible, you should head it off by acknowledging the possibility by saying something like, "Even though I'm involved in the paving business, I want to be clear that my comments on the condition of our streets are made in my capacity as chairman of the chamber of commerce."

"No comment" is not a substitute for "I don't know." Only when you have a reasonable explanation for doing so, such as on advice from your lawyer, should you use the phrase "no comment." Even then you should always explain why you can't comment; never just say "no comment" and let it go at that. If the real answer is that you don't know, then admit that you don't know. Never try to fake it. In any situation, without exception, if you don't know the answer, say so. If the answer would require information you shouldn't be expected to have, say so and explain why you aren't the right person to deal with that particular question.

If you're being interviewed off-air for a radio or television show, remember that recorded interviews are usually edited to a predetermined length, so short answers are less likely to be omitted or pared down to a comment that misrepresents your intended meaning.

Although in most media situations you will know more about your subject than the interviewer, you must never adopt a superior attitude. A good journalist will have done a lot of homework and will have access to an amount of research that might astound you. Adopting a superior attitude may well result in setting yourself up for a hard fall.

Another thing to remember is that the interviewer may have a biased opinion on a particular subject. It's not a good idea to get into an argument with the person holding the microphone, or who, as the old saying goes, buys ink by the barrel. But if you're asked a question that's based on an incorrect premise, always set the record straight before you respond.

Suppose you're the chief financial officer of a corporation and the journalist asks, "Why should we trust your financial statements when you can put anything in them you want to?" Before answering why your statements are trustworthy, you need to say something like, "I'm afraid you've been misinformed. Not only are there laws governing what we have to report, but our financial statements are authenticated by independent auditors."

Sometimes a journalist's question will contain inflammatory words or phrases. When this happens, don't legitimize and reinforce such words or phrases by repeating them in your answer; rephrase them into factual terms. If a journalist says your company is "irresponsible and a blight on your industry," don't reply by saying, "We are not irresponsible and a blight on our industry." Instead, say something like, "Well, what's really happening is that we're taking the following actions to . . . ," and go on to explain your position in a positive light. Or you can point out that the question is loaded by saying something like, "Well, you obviously disagree with us on this, but here are the facts," then go into your positive reply.

When you run into a confrontational question, keep your answer as short as possible. Don't stick both feet in your mouth by giving a long, rambling answer; you're apt to sound like you're protesting a tough question, and you might say something totally inappropriate. However, simple "yes" and "no" answers tend to be viewed as evasive and impolite. Say what you need to say and then shut up. Silence is never your problem; even on live radio or television, it's the interviewer's job to keep the show moving, not yours.

Be likeable, brief, honest, and positive. The reasons are simple. If you come across as an arrogant ass, the whole purpose of the press conference or the interview—usually to win the public's interest in your product or undertaking—will be negated. Talking too much endears you to nobody and increases the possibility of saying something inappropriate. If you're dishonest, you will be caught out, if not right away, then certainly later. Being positive pays off; nobody likes to watch and listen to negative, whining, complaining people.

Don't be rushed into poorly considered or incomplete answers because the journalist has a deadline. Again, that's the journalist's problem, not yours. Although short answers are preferable to long ones, you cannot adequately deal with a complicated issue in a seven-second sound bite.

It's easy to get into trouble by making off-the-cuff comments that end up being recorded without your knowledge. Whenever you are around media people, always assume the microphones are live, the cameras are running, and notes are being taken, even if it looks like they aren't. Although there is a concept of "off the record," you shouldn't rely on it unless the ground rules have been clearly laid down beforehand and you have a good reason to completely trust the journalist. In fact, if a comment has any potential to get you into trouble and there's nothing to be gained from the journalist's hearing it from you, then you just shouldn't make it.

The vast majority of journalists are honest, hard-working people who really aren't out to get you. But every journalist's mission is, in part, to get information to which they may not be entitled. The journalist has nothing to lose by interviewing you, but you, and those you represent, could lose a lot by what you say or how you say it.

REMEMBER:

1. "No comment" is not a substitute for "I don't know" and should never be used without giving a reasonable explanation for doing so.
2. Recorded interviews are usually edited, so short answers are less likely to be omitted or misrepresented.

TO-DO LIST:

1. If you don't know the answer to a question, say so.
2. Don't be rushed into poorly considered or incomplete answers; silence, the next question, and deadlines (real or imagined) are the journalist's problems, not yours.

3. Always assume there's an open mike or a running camera, and that notes are being taken.

4. Don't rely on the concept of "off the record" unless it's clearly defined beforehand and you completely trust the journalist.

5. Don't underestimate the amount of research a journalist may have done; adopting a superior attitude will only set you up for a fall.

6. Although it's never a good idea to get into an argument with an interviewer, always set the record straight when confronted with an incorrect premise.

7. Don't legitimize inflammatory words or phrases by repeating them in your answer.

8. Avoid long, rambling answers, but remember that "yes" and "no" answers are usually seen as being evasive and impolite.

9. Be likeable, brief, honest, and positive.

BETTER TO BE
LOOKED OVER
THAN OVERLOOKED

If you are like most people, there are few things in life
that will strike more fear into your heart than to be enjoy-
ing yourself at a wedding, retirement party, or community event and then suddenly realizing that the master of
ceremonies' sentence that began with, "And now, ladies
and gentlemen, we'll have a few words from . . ." has
ended with your name. Or similarly, finding yourself in
a meeting where you thought the sole purpose of your
attendance would be to listen to what others have to say
and being unexpectedly asked for your views.

The prospect of having to make impromptu remarks
often paralyzes even seasoned speakers; no one likes to
be made, unexpectedly and unwillingly, the centre of
attention. But there's really no need for panic. In fact,
you should welcome these occasions, because in the overall scheme of becoming a successful person, it's always
better to be looked over than it is to be overlooked.

Just think about it for a moment. The settings in
which you're most likely to be asked to make a few

impromptu remarks, such as weddings, retirement parties, and meetings, are all gatherings in which you will always have relevant personal experiences and knowledge to share. At a wedding reception or retirement party, you're not going to be called upon to say a few words unless you have some history with the newlyweds, the retiree or their families. And, as far as meetings are concerned, even if your attendance was mandated rather than purely voluntary, you wouldn't be there if you had no interest whatsoever in the topic being discussed; in fact, you'd probably have a keen interest in the subject.

You will always be able to adequately acquit yourself by simply thinking on your feet, which will be no problem if you follow the advice contained in this chapter. In no time at all you'll easily overcome whatever fear you might harbour when called on to make impromptu remarks.

There are two other reasons why you should never get too flustered about having to make some impromptu remarks. First, masters of ceremonies really mean it when they say "a few words." You actually shouldn't speak for more than one to three minutes, and you can succeed quite nicely by telling a story about the friend who's getting married or retiring. Similarly, if you aren't formally on the agenda at a meeting but do get called upon, you can always get by with making one point, backed up with a couple of examples, indicating why you feel the way you do. Second, in these circumstances the audience or your colleagues aren't going to hold you to a very high standard because they will empathize with your having been put on the spot. As mentioned, at the social event just tell an anecdote or two, and at the meeting make a salient point, and your reputation will be enhanced.

But what if hearing your name being called momentarily paralyzes your brain? Well, there are two effective methods for dealing with this situation. One will work almost every time, and the other will work *every* time. The reason I'm giving you both is that you may sometimes forget about the sure-fire method and will have to fall back on the almost foolproof one. We'll deal with the almost foolproof method first.

As already mentioned, in any impromptu speaking situation, you will always have enough knowledge of the topic to enable you to say *something*, you will very likely care in some way about the subject, and you can easily rationalize wanting to say a few words, if for no other reason than to avoid the embarrassment of not doing so. Therefore, all the elements of the formula for a successful talk, as outlined in Chapter 17, are present.

In the social situations, you will always have a few moments to organize your thoughts. If necessary, you can extend your thinking-on-your-feet time with the humorous "Who, me?" reaction. You can create even more thinking time by making your way slowly to the podium or to the front of the room, and you can always pause for few more seconds when you get there. In a meeting you can buy some more thinking time, if necessary, by asking a clarifying question or two.

During this thinking time ask yourself, "What can I say about this person or topic?" as the case might be. Usually the very first thought that comes into your mind is all that you will need to get you going. If the subject is a person, your first thought will probably be about something that happened involving at least two of you who are in the room. Just tell that story by answering the classic journalistic questions: What happened? Who was involved? Why did it happen? When did it happen? Where did it happen? How did it happen? Or, at the meeting, ask yourself, "How do I feel about this topic?"; "Why do I feel this way?"; and "What illustrations or examples can I use to back up my views?"

Now let's look at the foolproof method. Although quite simple to describe, the foolproof method for a successful impromptu speaking experience does require a bit of work, which is why most people neglect to use it. Here it is: Any time you know that you're going to be in a situation where there is any possibility whatsoever, no matter how remote, of being asked to "say a few words," decide beforehand exactly what you're going to say if called upon.

For example, if you're going to a wedding reception or a retirement party, think about a story you could tell if asked to speak, and go over in your mind some of the details that you would include. If you're going to be attending a meeting, review the agenda, think about how you feel about each item, and decide what points you'd make should the opportunity arise, and what illustrations and examples you could use to back up your position. Although it's perfectly in order to jot down a few notes, if you're called upon, don't refer to them when you are speaking. To do so, especially at a social occasion, would spoil the spontaneity of the occasion, raise the audience's expectations, and, very likely, reduce its appreciation of your ability to think on your feet.

Earning the reputation as a person who can think on his feet will enhance your reputation as a leader and communicator, as well as increase your overall confidence in handling unexpected situations, all of which will contribute enormously to your achieving success.

Once you get accustomed to using the techniques outlined above, don't be surprised if you become disappointed any time you're overlooked rather than being looked over.

REMEMBER:

1. Having to unexpectedly say a few words can happen any time you're in a group of people, but you'll rarely be asked to do so in a setting where you aren't adequately qualified to comply.

2. "A few words" is literally all that's wanted from you, so you only have to speak for a minute or two to fulfill your obligation.

3. The expectations of the audience in these circumstances aren't very high, so there isn't a lot of pressure on you.

4. All impromptu speaking requirements can be met by either telling a story or making a single point. Just ask yourself, "What can I say about this person or this topic?" and then expand on the first thing that comes to mind.

5. Earning the reputation as a person who is good at thinking on his feet will enhance your reputation as a leader and communicator.

TO-DO LIST:

1. Any time you're going to be in a situation where there's even a remote possibility of having to "say a few words," give some thought to what you would say if asked.

WHEN YOU'RE IN THE CHAIR, BE IN CHARGE

Just as most people will go through life without ever having to deal with the media, many people may never have occasion to chair a meeting; but many will, either in their careers or volunteer situations, or both.

Giving an effective presentation to a group of people increases your overall confidence and enhances your reputation as a leader; gaining recognition as a person who effectively chairs meetings will do the same. When you're in the chair, you're expected to be in charge, so make sure you are. This chapter tells you how.

Although you never want to be seen as an officious or inflexible chairperson, you should acquire some knowledge of the fundamental rules of parliamentary procedure, such as dealing with formal motions, accepting motions from the floor, debating protocol, how to close off a debate, and voting procedures. You can learn everything you need to know by picking up a copy of *Robert's Rules of Order*.

Consistently adhering to the following rules will ensure that you run effective and efficient meetings.

- Control the seating. Arrange for people who tend to argue with each other to sit on the same side of the table. Confrontations will be fewer and shorter if the potential combatants aren't facing each other across the table.
- Start on time, even if there is only one other person there. It won't take many meetings for your message to get through, and the number of latecomers will diminish with each meeting.
- Open with a brief statement of what you expect to accomplish, announce the time of adjournment, and stick to it.
- Ask if attendees are expecting any emergency messages on their cellphones, pagers, or PDAs. Suggest that anyone who isn't expecting a critical message turn off her device or, at the very minimum, turn it to "vibrate," and leave the room if she has to receive a transmission.
- Determine if anyone has any new business to add to the agenda. If there isn't enough time to deal with an item of new business, either the item of new business or an existing agenda item will have to be deferred. Arrive at and announce the decision right away.

- Be confident and enthusiastic, but remember that it's your responsibility to keep the meeting moving, on schedule, and on topic.
- Watch your tone of voice and body language; you always want to convey an image of leadership and of being in control. Even if your superiors are in attendance, you need to stay in control and should defer to them only in matters that are clearly outside your authority.
- Keep breaks to a minimum, but never go more than two hours without giving the attendees at least a chance to stretch their legs.
- Listen intently to all speakers.
- Don't introduce your own thoughts on an agenda item until it's obvious no one else is going to raise your points. An effective way to do this is to raise them as questions; that way you don't step out of your role as chair.
- Encourage everyone to participate, but never embarrass or force anyone into speaking.
- Don't let anyone dominate the discussion.
- Make brief notes of key points; don't simply rely on the secretary's minutes being as complete as you'd like them to be.
- Finish on time.
- Tell the participants when they can expect to receive minutes of the meeting, and make sure the minutes are distributed as promised.

- Be sure the minutes clearly outline the actions required and who is responsible for the actions being taken.

REMEMBER:

1. Gaining a reputation as a person who runs effective meetings will increase your self-confidence and enhance your reputation as a leader.

TO-DO LIST:

1. Acquire some knowledge of the fundamentals of parliamentary procedure.
2. Until they become second nature to you, never chair a meeting without reviewing the rules set out in this chapter.

TO BECOME A
PARTNER IN YOUR FIRM,
ACT LIKE ONE

This chapter will be of interest mainly to those who work in professional firms. Although professionals such as accountants, lawyers, architects, and other consultants are allowed to incorporate in nearly all jurisdictions, most firms still operate, in effect, as partnerships. This chapter will also be of interest to entrepreneurs who, although operating under the umbrella of a corporation, carry on business in a manner that has most of the characteristics of a professional partnership.

Even though most young professionals joining such organizations have the goal of becoming a partner, the majority of them will not.

In some cases it's a numbers game that prevents perfectly qualified individuals from realizing their dream; there are simply too many good candidates looking to fill too few partner slots. Some people don't make partner because they don't sufficiently develop their technical skills. Others simply choose not to become partners because they're unwilling to take on the potential financial liability and the inherent expanded responsibilities of partnership. But far too often, aspiring young professionals are excluded from partnership because they don't master the art of being proficient and effective business partners.

The art of being a proficient and effective business partner comprises a complex mix of skills and attitudes, but they are skills and attitudes that can be learned and developed. Described below, in no particular order because their importance changes depending on the particular circumstances, are the most important skills and attitudes that need to be developed before you can become a proficient, effective, and appreciated business partner.

- Partners need to understand that they own the business and that its future depends on their continuing to build its customer and client base; no one else is going to do it for them. Partners need to always take the unselfish, long-term view when making important decisions, meaning that individual sacrifices often need to be made for the overall good of the firm.
- Partners need to have the confidence to evaluate and the courage to act; if you want to be a partner in your firm, you can't abstain from taking part in difficult decisions and executing the solutions, no matter how unpleasant some of them

may be. As a partner, you can't spend too much time worrying about the possible negative results of a tough decision. The burdens of partnership will always include being unpopular from time to time.

- Because not all of your ideas are going to be accepted all of the time, you have to be able to take "no" for an answer without becoming angry or discouraged. You also have to be able to accept criticism without becoming overly defensive. It's at times like these that a good sense of humour will prove to be a valuable asset that's particularly appreciated by your colleagues.

- No one can be all things to all people all the time, so you have to learn to trust your partners. It's equally important to understand that even people you trust will occasionally let you down, and when this happens you need to react with the same graciousness you would want to receive if you were the one who dropped the ball.

- As a partner, you have to be able to keep your spirits up when things go wrong, not only for the sake of the other partners, but also for the sake of the firm's staff and clients. You need to be able to keep completely cool in emergencies and bolster their enthusiasm no matter how difficult a particular set of circumstances may be. Partners understand that assigning blame doesn't solve a problem, so they never waste time trying to find something or somebody to blame; they just get on with the task at hand.

- All partners in a firm need to play some sort of leadership role, which basically means having a clear idea of their main function in the organization and how they are expected to further the fortunes of the firm by getting others to follow their lead. Effective partners are able to motivate staff members to do superior work by inspiring them to reach their potential. They also need to be able to persuade customers and clients to follow the firm's recommendations. To do this, partners must have a deep understanding of how people feel and what influences them, as well as a great deal of diplomacy and tact.
- Partners should have above-average communication skills, and must be able to effectively chair meetings.
- Although partners must always respect the rights and worth of everyone, and never treat staff as inferior, they also understand that not everyone they hire will be able to meet the standards required, and that sometimes people just have to be let go. If their key people aren't top-notch, when the firm is in a difficult situation, it will not have top-notch people to help get out of it.

In addition to the partnership qualities listed above, I've identified ten good working habits that effective partners in professional firms all seem to have.

- Be approachable and easy to talk to.
- Always listen with a view to understanding what the other person is actually saying, not simply with a view to deciding what *you're* going to say.
- Never pass up an opportunity to show appreciation to others or to make them feel important.
- Check the business section of your paper every morning before starting work. At the very minimum, peruse it for references to your clients or your firm.
- Remember that even if you can't do *everything* right now, you can do *something* right now.
- Make notes; the strongest memory is weaker than the palest ink.
- Be sure your schedule always has room for the unexpected, as well as some time for you to think.
- Spend at least one hour a week networking.
- Always dress just a *little* better than the occasion calls for.
- Read something at least twice a week that's outside your field.

All of the advice contained in this chapter can be summed up in one sentence: If you want to become a partner in your firm, then start acting like one.

REMEMBER:

1. Many people don't become partners in professional firms simply because they never mastered the art of being effective partners.

TO-DO LIST:

1. Understand that you own the business and that its future depends on you.
2. Have the confidence to evaluate and the courage to act; understand that being a partner means being unpopular from time to time.
3. Be able to take "no" for an answer without becoming discouraged.
4. Be able to accept criticism without becoming angry.
5. Let your sense of humour show.
6. Trust your partners, but realize that even people you trust will let you down occasionally.
7. Keep your spirits up when things go wrong.
8. Develop the ten good habits of effective partners listed in this chapter.

22

TALENT ALONE WON'T DO IT

It's always an advantage to be more talented and better informed than other people in your field, but it's rarely in your best interest to tell them so. As critical to your success as talent is, when dealing with people, diplomacy and tact can be even more important in achieving success.

At a dinner party or cocktail gathering, when someone starts spouting off on something that you know more about than they do, don't feel that you always have to set the record straight.

Whether you've made more money in the stock market, closed a bigger deal, solved a more difficult problem, or simply had a more serious bout of the flu than someone is describing, it's best to just keep quiet unless you're asked about your experiences. Even then, you should keep your comments short, to the point, and noncondescending, letting other people have their say without seeming to upstage them.

We can make more enemies by what we say (and how we say it) than friends by what we do. When diplomacy and tact are called for, words need to be chosen carefully and tone of voice has to be controlled.

You cannot be diplomatic and tactful when you're being rude. When you're rude, you're telling people they don't matter; when you're nice to people, you're telling them that they do. Nor is being miserable or resentful very tactful. Beating others at politeness is always a diplomatic victory.

Sometimes people inadvertently become undiplomatic and abandon tact. Be careful—comments you think are frank and candid might actually be thoughtless and cruel. Sometimes when we speak "straight from the heart," that message bypasses the brain. Support your beliefs by all means, but never ridicule other people's.

In some situations, silence is often the best comment; if something "goes without saying," let it. Silence is also sometimes the only satisfactory substitute for knowledge; if you don't know what you're talking about, it's always better to keep quiet. Most people know *how* to say nothing; diplomacy and tact are about knowing *when* to say nothing.

One of the times when your diplomacy and tact need to be carefully exercised is when you have to say "no" to someone. Deceit is not a synonym for tact, so a civil "no" accompanied by a gentle explanation is always better than an insincere "yes" that you have no intention of living up to. For example, a diplomatic way to say "no" to something you don't want to do is to say, "I'm sorry, but I can't commit to that because there are some other things that I simply have to tend to instead."

A great test of diplomacy and tact is to know how to do something really well and, without comment, watch someone else doing it in an ineffective manner. As long as the other person isn't going to irreparably mess things up, it's not worth hurting someone's feelings, and perhaps damaging a relationship, by jumping in and demonstrating your superior talent.

But of course there are times when criticism is necessary. For example, if you observe an employee doing something in an inefficient manner, you should always show that person the better way to do it; or, if someone is endangering himself or others by his behaviour, you should always step in. People who don't criticize when they should are as wrong as those who never give praise.

The mistake that a lot of people make when they have to criticize someone is thinking that this is the time to set aside diplomacy and tact. If you want your criticism to be effective, nothing could be further from the truth. Criticizing someone is precisely the time when you should be as diplomatic and tactful as possible. A good rule of thumb is that if you're looking forward to criticizing someone, don't start your tongue until you get your diplomacy and tact gears engaged; only then will you be ready to do it right. When it comes to criticism, use your head to criticize yourself, your heart to criticize others.

If you are a regular bridge player, you will have had lots of opportunities to observe fruitless criticism. I learned first-hand while playing bridge that when offering criticism, we should always refer to the fault, not the person. After my partner had made a bid that cost us a lot of points, I blurted out, "You know, that was a really stupid bid." What my partner heard was, "You're really stupid!" The enjoyment quickly went out of the game. On the other hand, if I had calmly said, "There's another bid that might have been better there," everyone would have continued to enjoy the game and my partner would actually have learned something. Remember, too, that there are times to blink as well as to see; being diplomatic and tactful sometimes merely consists of knowing what to overlook. Before you embark on criticism, be sure it really is necessary and will have constructive results. In a fun bridge game, advice should never be given unless it's asked for; I should have just kept quiet.

Don't let anyone hear your criticism of them secondhand. If you need to discuss a particular situation with a third party, don't do so until you've met with the person who will be the subject of your criticism and let him know how you feel. Whenever possible, your criticism should be delivered in person and in private. Face-to-face criticism is always more effective than an email, telephone call, or memo, and you will rarely be effective when you criticize someone in front of others.

One way to help keep your criticism constructive is to deliver it along with recommendations for improvement. Also, be sure that all your comments are necessary; when something you'd really like to say can't possibly do any good, don't say it.

Criticism, even when it's not intended to be, can be a humiliating experience for the recipient. The next time you have to criticize someone, before doing so, take a moment to remember the last time that you were criticized and how you felt.

Of course, criticism is a two-sided coin; you might be the deliverer or you might be the receiver. There are three important points to remember when you find yourself on the receiving end of criticism.

- Criticism from a wise person beats praise from a fool.
- Never resent criticism. Just as with unsolicited advice, if the criticism is not justified, you can ignore it, and if it is justified, you can learn from it.
- When someone seems to be criticizing you unreasonably, he may just be mad at himself.

REMEMBER:

1. More enemies are made by what we say than are friends by what we do.

2. When you're rude, you're telling people they don't matter; when you're nice to them, you're telling them they do.

3. Being miserable or resentful is never very diplomatic, and beating others at politeness is always a great victory.

4. Silence is often the best comment. If something "goes without saying," let it; you don't always have to set the record straight.

5. Deceit is not a synonym for tact; learn how to say "no" diplomatically.

6. It's a great test of diplomacy and tact when you know how to do something really well and, without comment, you watch somebody else doing it badly.

7. But there are times when criticism is necessary; people who don't criticize when they should are no better than those who never praise.

8. If it will hurt you to criticize someone, you'll probably do it right. If you're looking forward to it, consciously bring your diplomatic skills into play.

TO-DO LIST:

1. Be sure that frank and candid isn't really just thoughtless and cruel.
2. Use your head to criticize yourself, your heart to criticize others.
3. Criticize the fault, not the person.
4. There are times to blink as well as to see; be sure any criticism is necessary and constructive.
5. Never let anyone hear your criticism second-hand.
6. Deliver your criticism in person and in private.
7. Before criticizing someone's actions, know clearly what alternative you're going to suggest.
8. When something you'd really like to say can't possibly do any good, say nothing.
9. The next time you're about to criticize someone, remember the last time you were criticized.
10. When receiving criticism, keep it in perspective.

THE ONLY WAY TO NEVER MAKE MISTAKES IS TO NEVER MAKE DECISIONS

One of the most important skills required to achieve success, right up there with the ability to communicate, is the ability to make decisions. Certainly the highest-paid executives are all excellent decision-makers.

Good decision-makers don't fear being wrong occasionally because they know that the only way to never make a mistake is to never make a decision. They also know that if they never make decisions, they seldom get anything done.

You will not always be able to completely control the results of your decisions, but you can usually keep control of the process; and make no mistake about it, there is a definite decision-making process.

The most important step in the decision-making process is to wait until your emotions are in neutral before taking any action. Decisions made in the midst of an overwhelming emotional reaction—be it enthusiasm, anger, sorrow, humiliation, or other—often turn out to be completely inappropriate. Following are examples of bad non-executive decisions I've seen people make while in the throes of emotion. (It would take a separate book to catalogue all the bad executive decisions I've seen made when people are overly emotional.)

- Enthusiasm: vastly overpaying for a residence without engaging in enough research, inspection, introspection, or consideration of future requirements, then having to sell it at a substantial loss.
- Anger: more bad decisions are made in anger than any other emotional experience, such as the professional hockey player who cost himself a small fortune in lost income, legal fees, and possible damages (the lawsuits are still ongoing at the time of writing), not to mention the damage to his own career, because he decided in anger to assault another player, resulting in the end of that player's career.
- Sorrow: a new widow selling her home and moving to another city away from family and friends, only to have to move back a couple of years later after much emotional and financial cost.
- Humiliation: a young chartered accounting student lashing out at her boss during an office party because the boss had made, in front of others, what the student took to be a disparaging remark about her background. The outburst poisoned

their relationship to the point where the student had to change firms, considerably delaying her career advancement.

The second most important step in the decision-making process is to gather as much information as you can before coming to your conclusion. Decisions are rarely any better than the intelligence on which they are based. A key aspect of getting the information you need to make a sound decision is to ask questions. I've rarely, if ever, regretted asking a question, whereas there've been many times when I've regretted not asking one.

While gathering your information, you have to remain objective. Ignoring facts doesn't change them; reality has to be faced. It's not what you would like the situation to be that matters; it's what the situation actually is that has to be dealt with. For example, if in gathering the facts you learn that your company doesn't have the resources to follow through on a particular course of action, then a decision to follow a different one has to be made.

The best formula for gathering the information necessary to make a decision that I've ever come across was one I learned when I took the Dale Carnegie course. It was a five-step process that went something like this:

- State the problem as simply as possible.
- List all the causes of the problem.

- List every possible solution, no matter how "far out" it might be (which is called "brainstorming" today).
- Pick the best possible solution.
- Decide how to make that solution happen.

Taking the time to go through these steps will help ensure that your emotions are in check and that you've gathered sufficient information on which to base a decision.

During the decision-making process, you need to separate facts from opinions, and you should always give more weight to the facts. Everyone is entitled to have an opinion, but it's good to keep in mind that just because an opinion is held by a certain person, no matter how influential, that alone doesn't make it a fact. Another thing to remember is that facts are like stories: they exist in a specific context and might not have the same use to us in another. So-called facts should always be examined carefully to determine their relevance and probable impact in the particular context of the problem you're dealing with. It's rare for two situations to be identical, but if they are, be sure to determine what the outcome was in the previous situation. Somebody once defined stupidity as making the same decision and expecting a different result.

Another distinction that you have to make in the decision-making process is the difference between a prediction and a fantasy. Just because you would dearly love something to happen doesn't mean that it will. You have to recognize that your feelings and personal experiences may not be typical of the population as a whole, so other people's reactions to your decision may well be the opposite of what you would like them to be. For example, before deciding to start a business based on a new product or service that you would use personally, be sure that you've done sufficient research to determine whether others think as highly of the product as you do. Only then can you reasonably estimate whether a sufficiently wide market actually exists.

The next issue to be faced in the decision-making process is timing. The most important timing consideration is avoiding the two extremes: unwarranted delay on the one hand, and impulsive, snap decisions on the other. When being pressured into making a quick decision, the best answer is always "no." This is because it's usually easier to change a "no" to a "yes" than vice versa. Never rush a decision if there's no compelling reason to do so.

But indecision is not desirable either. When considering the consequences of an action, always factor in the consequences of inaction. A well thought-out and timely decision is like a scalpel that cuts clean and straight, while indecision is like a dull knife that causes ragged gashes. With a well thought-out decision, you're on your way to a successful operation; indecision, on the other hand, results in unnecessary delays in getting on with the operation, and the patient's unattended-to problems getting worse.

One form of indecision involves spending too much time considering a back-up position. Concentrate too long on your back-up position and you may well end up needing it, because the opportunity to execute your preferred action may have passed. As a colleague of mine once put it, stare at anything long enough and it'll start making faces at you.

Even though all of the aforementioned aspects of decision-making are important, you should be careful not to over-complicate the decision-making process. Simple solutions may have to be discarded, but they should always be considered first. When instinct and logic both clearly suggest the same decision, it's probably the right decision.

The final step in the decision-making process is deciding how to turn your decision into action, which should always include deciding how, and to whom, you are going to communicate the decision. As is the case in all important communications, you need to state your decision not just so that it can be clearly understood, but also so that it cannot be misunderstood. Therefore, the communication must be carefully crafted and should always point out the benefits of the decision to the people involved, as well as exactly what will be expected from them in its implementation.

There are three more aspects of decision-making to keep in mind.

The first is that you have to practise making decisions; mastering the decision-making process gets easier the more you do it. People will remember how you handled a problem long after they've forgotten what the problem was.

The second is that you cannot be right all the time; when you get a mouthful of scalding hot coffee, whatever you do next is going to be wrong. Although it would be nice to always be able to do everything right, sometimes you just have to do what can be done.

Finally, it's always better to be someone dealing with a problem than it is to be a problem that someone else has to deal with, which can happen if you take too long making a decision.

REMEMBER:

1. You may not be able to completely control the results of a decision, but you *can* keep control of the process.
2. Your decisions will be no better than the information on which they are based; the first step in getting the answers you need is to ask questions.
3. Facts, like stories, exist in a context and should always be examined to determine their appropriateness in your particular situation.

4. A well thought-out decision is a scalpel that cuts clean and straight; indecision is a dull knife that leaves ragged gashes.

5. Your personal feelings and experiences aren't necessarily typical of the population as a whole.

6. The person who must know the perfect result before deciding usually never decides.

7. Simple solutions may not turn out to be the right ones, but they should always be considered first.

8. When instinct and logic suggest the same decision, it's probably the right decision.

9. The more decisions you make, the better you become at making them.

10. No one is going to be right all the time; sometimes you just have to do what can be done.

11. People will remember how you dealt with a problem long after they've forgotten what the problem was.

TO-DO LIST:

1. Don't make a decision until your emotions are in neutral.

2. Eliminate options that would result in consequences you can't live with.

3. Remain objective. Ignoring facts doesn't change them; reality has to be faced.

4. Give facts more weight than opinions.
5. Avoid the two extremes when timing your decision: unwarranted delay and an impulsive, snap decision.
6. Never rush a decision when there's no real need to.
7. When pressured into making a quick decision, the best answer is always "no," because it's easier to turn a "no" into a "yes" than vice versa.
8. When considering the consequences of an action, always consider the consequences of inaction.

WHO YOU KNOW IS IMPORTANT AND SO IS WHO KNOWS YOU

Business executives and professionals know that networking is one of the most cost-effective and efficient marketing tools available. They also know that the non-marketing benefits of an effective network can be important to their personal success, such as when they're trying to hire someone or when they're looking for jobs themselves. An effective network can also provide resources on which they can call to help them solve problems or obtain all kinds of useful information. Networking also means that many people know who you are and what you have to offer.

There are three reasons why most people don't network effectively. The first is the mistaken view held by many (including some short-sighted employers) that networking is an unprofessional and self-serving activity. Nothing could be further from the truth. If you're networking effectively, you're as apt to help someone else as you are to be helped yourself and, when done properly, networking is a perfectly socially acceptable activity that can be professionally satisfying for all concerned. To achieve success, particularly in the business world, who you know is important, and it's equally important who knows you. I once heard it put this way: you need to know who you need to know before you need to know them.

The second reason people fail to develop an effective network is that they give up too easily when their networking efforts don't seem to be paying off. Networking success, just like any other success, is rarely achieved by a single action. Networking is almost always a long-term project; although you may occasionally reap instant rewards, it could take a long time for your networking to show results. But the rewards, when they do come, are worth the effort and the wait.

The third reason why people fail in their networking efforts is that they don't really know how to do it. That's what the rest of this chapter is about.

The best possible networking technique is helping others achieve their goals. But to do that you have to develop your network, watch for opportunities to help people in it, and then help them. This takes a combination of time, effort, and diplomacy. You need to tactfully gather useful information about the people in your network. You also need to tactfully let people know what your strengths and interests are so that they'll be comfortable asking you for information or advice. In some cases, you shouldn't even wait to be asked. If you come across some information that would be of particular interest to someone in your network and you are reasonably sure they don't have it, send it to them.

Useful information to gather about members of your network (always with an eye to discovering mutual interests) includes place of work; position; address; telephone, fax, pager, and cell numbers; email address; birthday and anniversary dates; spouse's name; details of children; hobbies; sports; preferred reading material; and type of music enjoyed. Never hesitate to share the same personal information about yourself in return.

Some especially diligent networkers keep a "last contact" note for each person in their network, indicating when, how, and why the contact took place, as well as what was discussed, what follow-ups were required, the outcome, and when and how the next contact will be made.

When networking—whether in person, on the telephone, or in writing—you always have to look, act, and sound like a person who's worth knowing. So be sure to comport yourself in a professional manner, always being gracious and courteous.

You need to develop a networking plan, covering such items as deciding which organizations you're going to join, how often you're going to lunch with people and with whom, how many and which cocktail parties you're going to attend, how you're going to organize the information you gather about people, when you will call them, when you will drop them a note, and how much time and money you will devote to networking. Work hard to make networking a habit, and work even harder at finding opportunities to help people in your network.

When considering the role of industry and trade organizations or service clubs in your networking plan, remember that it's far better to actively work one organization than to passively belong to twenty. Join committees and be quick to volunteer.

A lot of effective networking can be done on the telephone and by email. But be sure you do it appropriately and in a timely fashion; you never want to be seen as a pest. If you're going to call or email someone in your network, be sure there's a reason. "Just touching base" isn't a reason; an invitation to lunch or to an event is, as would be a legitimate request for information or advice. Because people receive so many unsolicited emails, you should use emails judiciously in your networking. It's always in order to use email to respond to another person's email or to forward items of interest to people.

Keep on the lookout for opportunities to drop personal notes to people in your network, such as birthday or anniversary greetings or to acknowledge an accomplishment. In these situations, handwritten notes on good-quality stationery stand out and are superior to emails.

When you receive an email, you usually know what the subject matter is and you're able to take some time to formulate your response. However, when you pick up a phone message, you don't always know what the person was calling about. Although you should return calls as soon as possible, if you know what's going be discussed, take some time to think about what you're going to say. If you don't know what the discussion is going to be about, it's a good idea to take a little time to review what you know about the person and give some thought as to what the subject matter might be.

Re-evaluate your network on a regular basis; not everyone you meet will necessarily be a part of an effective and efficient network, and from time to time you will have to remove some people from your networking circle. On the other hand, you never know when you will run into a person whose association should be cultivated. Consider the following list of potential networking sources: friends, neighbours, bank manager, insurance agent, accountant, lawyer, investment advisor, investment club, service clubs, professional and industry associations, schools (yours and your children's), sports (yours and your children's), past and present clients, suppliers, seatmates (at events or when travelling), and alumni associations.

Although sporting events and dinner parties can sometimes be useful networking venues, the prime networking opportunities occur at conferences, conventions, and cocktail parties.

Even though the cocktail party has long been the classic networking venue, it's also the most misused. While many of the following points apply equally to coffee breaks at conventions and seminars, for ease of presentation we'll deal with them in the context of the cocktail party.

Most people make their first networking mistake as soon as they walk into the room. They look around for friends or colleagues to talk to. That's not networking, that's visiting.

What you should do is look around to see if there's anyone standing off alone. That person has an immediate need that you can fill; he is very likely feeling at least a little bit uncomfortable and will welcome someone to talk to, if for no other reason than to feel less conspicuous. That's who you should head for; introduce yourself and strike up a conversation. Even if the other person is waiting for someone to arrive, you can't lose. You've already made a contact, done him or her a favour, and when the awaited person arrives, you'll be given another introduction. In that situation, once you've politely acknowledged the new arrival and exchanged some pleasantries, it's time to move on; you don't want to become an intruder.

If there's no one standing off by himself, then it's perfectly fine to say hello to people you know, but keep your peripheral vision peeled for the lonely arrival, and head for that person as soon as you can politely do so. As already emphasized, it's best to approach a single person and it's certainly in order to approach a group of three or more, but stay away from pairs. You may be a saviour to the single person standing off in the corner or simply another person in a group, but to two people already engaged in a conversation, you're an interruption. So stay away from pairs unless invited to join them or someone else joins them. You might also consider becoming the lonely waif and gamble on someone approaching you so that you can work the technique in reverse.

Never go to a cocktail party without a good supply of business cards, some paper, and a pen. People tend to keep business cards—some have a drawer full of them—and most people actually refer to them from time to time. Even if they're sorting through their business cards to decide which ones they're going to throw away, they'll see yours. If you made a good impression, they'll probably keep the card. If the people you're talking to haven't asked for a business card by the time you're parting company, ask for one of theirs and offer one of yours. Be on the lookout for opportunities to give people a business card, such as writing the title of a book you've been discussing on the back of it, or the name of a restaurant you've recommended. A good networker can usually ensure that anyone they've been talking to for the first time leaves with one of their business cards. It's worth repeating: every time someone looks at your business card he's being reminded of you, which is what networking is all about.

You need paper and pen to note what you've learned about the people you've met for the first time, and any relevant new information regarding people already in your network. Some of the information you need will be on new contacts' business cards, but you need to make notes about other things you learn, such as spouses' names, children's names and ages, hobbies and recreation, what they like to read, the kind of music they like, what sports they follow, and perhaps their birthdays and anniversaries. (Incidentally, these are all good topics of conversation, but as mentioned in Chapter 14, it's best to stay away from bear traps such as politics and religion when talking to people you don't know well.)

You should make your notes as soon as possible, while the information is still fresh in your mind; the only thing worse than not having enough information is having the wrong information. Make the notes as soon as you get in your car to go home or when you get back to your room if you're staying at a hotel. Perhaps a visit to the washroom before you leave the party will afford you the chance. In any event, make your notes some time before you go to bed that night. You can properly organize them the next day.

Now let's look at some things you should not do when networking.

Don't get into a feeding or drinking frenzy. You can't possibly be at your best balancing a drink and a heaping plate of food while frantically stuffing another mini-quiche in your mouth and trying to brush crumbs off your suit. Not exactly the image you want to convey, right?

Don't sit; people won't think you're tired from a hard day's work, they'll just think you're lazy. Even if you're still suffering from that skiing accident, you'll get more kudos and attention leaning on your crutches than you will slumped on a sofa with people tripping over your cast.

This may seem trivial, but it isn't: don't hold your drink in your right hand. Not only does it mean you will have to shift it to shake hands, but you'll be offering a cold, clammy hand.

Finally, the most important rule for networking: don't wait for things to happen; make them happen.

REMEMBER:

1. Networking is one of the most cost-effective, efficient marketing tools available to many executives and professionals.
2. An effective network is also important in non-marketing situations and can be critical to your business success.
3. When done properly, networking is perfectly socially acceptable and professionally satisfying.
4. As a member of an effective network, you're as apt to help someone else as you are to receive help.

5. Networking is a long-term project. Although you may occasionally reap an instant reward, it could take a long time. But the rewards, when they come, are worth the effort and the wait.

6. The best possible networking opportunity is helping others achieve their goals; find out how you can help and then do it.

TO-DO LIST:

1. Always be on the lookout for useful information and make a note of it as soon as you can.

2. Look, sound, and act like a person who's worth knowing.

3. Develop a networking plan.

4. Make networking a habit.

5. Actively work one organization rather than passively belonging to many.

6. Don't be a pest; be sure your calls, emails, and correspondence are appropriate and timely.

7. Re-evaluate your network on a regular basis, always looking out for new networking opportunities.

8. Until they become second nature to you, always review the suggestions in this chapter before attending cocktail parties, conventions, and seminars.

UNLESS YOU'RE THE LEAD DOG, THE VIEW IS ALWAYS THE SAME

Whatever the context—sports, business, community, or other—leadership implies a team situation with outstanding performances by an individual who inspires others to follow his or her lead. The best way to test your leadership ability is to check to see if anyone is following you. Without followers there is no leadership; to be a leader you must earn the right to have followers.

Leadership is not determined by title or position, nor is it determined by who you know. Leadership isn't even determined by what you know. Leadership comprises sound decision-making and effective actions. It's what you actually do, and how you do it, that determines how well you lead. But it isn't just the number of things you do that determines whether you're a leader; rather, it's the number of things you do well. Quality always counts more than quantity in determining leadership. You can demonstrate leadership skills in any situation, regardless of what your position or title might be. When you do so consistently, you will be considered a leader. And the view is always better when you're the lead dog.

Leaders have the ability to develop other people's skills and talents, and they are always willing to take the time to do so. Leaders are approachable and easy to talk to, always giving the impression that they have lots of time to spare. Even when they're overtaxed themselves, leaders will never brush off a person seeking advice or help. A true leader, if not able to deal with the situation right away, will explain why and arrange a strategy for dealing with it as soon as possible.

Leaders are able to get average people to do superior work by understanding how other people feel, knowing what motivates them, and always showing consideration for their feelings. They remember that results are achieved through reason and persuasion, not by ordering people around. As a result, people tend to try harder for effective leaders. It's the old rope principle. Pull a rope and it will follow you; push it and it will curl up and go nowhere. The same applies to being a strong leader of people. Effective leaders also never forget that even people who don't mind sharing credit still want and deserve to receive their fair share; effective leaders always make sure that they do.

Truly effective leadership produces new leaders as well as followers. This happens when leaders effectively delegate responsibility. And the best way to delegate responsibility is to let people know that you trust them.

People won't believe that you really trust them if you always try to control everything they do. Micro-managers are seldom perceived as real leaders. Real leaders help people do a better job without doing it for them. They act like coaches, not quarterbacks; they teach rather than take over, and always tell people how they're doing before being asked. Leaders not only have to be self-confident, they also have to inspire confidence in others.

If you want to be an effective leader, you have to become adept at dealing with problems. You can't worry too much about the possible negative results of your decisions; if you do, then you should be taking orders, not giving them. The burdens of leadership will always include being unpopular from time to time; leadership means doing what it is necessary, not simply doing what is popular. As difficult as it may be at times, to be an effective leader you have to keep your preconceptions in check and your personal likes and dislikes out of your decisions.

Keeping cool in emergencies and being able to make difficult things seem simple, rather than making simple things seem difficult, are earmarks of leadership. Leaders come up with solutions that are easily understood.

Leaders are good listeners and never hesitate to ask questions that non-leaders might not even realize should be asked, such as whether an employee is having a personal problem that the leader might be able to help with.

Effective leaders also have the diplomatic skills to ask such questions in a non-threatening way and without embarrassing the employee.

Leaders also recognize that the occasional disappointment is the price of progress, so they're able to take a "no" answer without becoming discouraged and can deal with disagreement without losing their tempers. And they don't equate disagreement with disloyalty; they're able to diplomatically turn a "why" situation into "why not?"

When the effective leader's work is done, everyone says, "*We* did it!"

REMEMBER:

1. The best test of leadership is to look around and see if anyone is following.
2. You must earn the right to have followers.
3. Leadership is action, not title or position.
4. Effective leadership produces other leaders as well as followers.
5. Leaders are not easily discouraged.
6. The effective delegation of responsibility is an important earmark of dynamic leadership.
7. The best way to delegate responsibility is to let people know that you trust them.
8. You don't have to control everything all the time.
9. Even people who don't mind sharing credit still want to get their fair share.

10. When the effective leader's work is done, everyone says, "We did it!"

TO-DO LIST:

1. Be willing to take the time to help develop the skills and talents of others.
2. Understand what influences people.
3. Show consideration for the feelings of others.
4. Get your results through reason and persuasion, not by ordering people around.
5. Help people do a better job, but don't do it for them.
6. Don't worry too much about the possible negative results of your decisions; leadership means doing what is necessary, not just what is popular.
7. Keep cool in emergencies.
8. Make difficult things seem simple, not simple things seem difficult.
9. Keep your preconceptions and personal likes and dislikes out of your decisions.
10. Never equate disagreement with disloyalty.

IT'S NOT THE CARDS
YOU HOLD, IT'S HOW
YOU PLAY THEM

You will never reach your full potential unless you become a successful negotiator, and skilled negotiators know that a successful negotiation comes not from the cards they hold but from the skillful playing of those cards. But you first have to deal yourself a hand.

The most common negotiating error is not made during the negotiation itself, but before the actual negotiation begins. The mistake is not preparing properly. Proper preparation is critical in determining the cards you will have available to play during the negotiation itself.

Of course you need to know everything there is to know about your own negotiating position and how you're going to make your case. The bigger problem is anticipating the other side's positions, how their cards will be played, and how you will respond. Put yourself in the other person's shoes and try to anticipate the points and objections that will be raised. Properly prepared negotiators are already ahead of the game.

Another key consideration in the playing of your negotiating cards is to find out as many facts about the situation as you can and examine them carefully. Determine whether there is some specific information that might make or break you, and if there is, decide how you're going to deal with it. Don't start actual negotiations until you completely understand all the issues. Until then, you should merely exchange information with the other side. You have to gain an understanding of the other side's needs and decide how you can fulfill at least some of them. Only an idiot holds out for absolutely everything.

You should only play your trump cards with people who can actually make decisions for the other side. If the person across the table from you can't make binding decisions, don't go beyond exchanging background and peripheral information. There's no point in making your key positions known to people who can't act on them.

In a negotiation, it's always more important to determine *what* is right than it is to determine *who* is right. Successful negotiators make sure the focus stays on solving the problem rather than defeating each other. Total win or total loss provides no options. When both sides respect each other, disagreements can remain a genuine effort to understand differences. You can't antagonize and persuade at the same time, so when you have to reject another person's idea, be sure to reject only the idea, not the person.

Always start a negotiation by listing the points of agreement. You have to accept what you believe to be true, even if it hurts your case, and you should never tamper with the truth.

In any negotiation, it's most effective to concentrate on the objective and then work backwards through the obstacles.

To the greatest extent possible, negotiate only one issue at a time. You can list all the points of disagreement, but each item should be dealt with in at least some degree of isolation. Otherwise, the issues could become so entangled that opportunites for compromise could be obscured, thereby prolonging the process unnecessarily. And compromise is what a negotiation is all about; otherwise, it's just a fight, not a negotiation.

If there's no room for discussion and concession, there's no room for negotiation. Another characteristic of negotiating to keep in mind in this context is that gaining something that is extremely unprofitable to the other side is apt to eventually be unprofitable to you, most probably by your having to make a larger concession later on.

The quality of your compromises will be more important in the long run than the quantity of your positions. By giving up a few points of lesser value, you will sometimes later win an extremely valuable point.

As already mentioned, in any successful negotiation, each side must determine the needs of the other and fulfill at least some of them. The exact needs of both sides are seldom the same, so it should be possible for both to "win" in a negotiation. The best solution to any conflict is one that helps both sides in some way, so the best way to "win" is to find a way in which the other side in a negotiation doesn't have to "lose."

You need a lot of patience to be an effective negotiator. It's rare to be able to obtain the best outcome quickly; speed usually means risk, so don't let the other side set the pace if you're uncomfortable with it. You should never play your real deadline card until you absolutely have to. Once the other side knows your real deadline, the pace of the negotiation is virtually set.

Just as you wouldn't let an opponent always deal the cards in a poker game, you shouldn't let the other side dominate the tone of a negotiation. As much as possible, discuss the issue in your terms and stay with your line of reasoning. Don't use the other side's language to describe a situation; always stick to your own terminology. However, you do have to tailor your arguments to take into consideration the personalities, attitudes, and experiences of those you are negotiating with. Always make your points in terms that the other side can relate to and understand.

Don't take the position that you know everything. Admitting that you don't have all the answers usually results in the other side's being more receptive to your suggestions.

Threats or ultimatums should only be used when the potential benefit is worth the possible cost. There's an old saying in the world of negotiation that recognized tactics aren't tactics. Whether playing an ultimatum card—saying "take what I'm now offering or no deal"—will work will depend on the other side's investment of time, money, and effort up to the point where the ultimatum is put on the table. Accordingly, an ultimatum should come near the end of a negotiation, not at the beginning. The main point in using leverage is not to overuse it. It's also rarely productive to make demands you'd never accept yourself; they may come back to haunt you later.

If the other side introduces a deal-breaker early in the negotiation, admit that it's a problem, but delay discussing it in detail as long as you can. You shouldn't relieve the other side's stress until you get something in return. This is a good time to point out that in any negotiation, silence can be an extremely powerful tool. The other side will usually be uncomfortable with your silence and may reveal some things it wouldn't have otherwise. Silence is pretty hard to rebut, so learn to master it.

Finally, know when to stop. When you have more to lose than you have to gain, it's clearly time to put away the cards.

REMEMBER:

1. Properly prepared negotiators are already ahead of the game.
2. It's always more important to determine what is right than it is to determine who is right.
3. The best solution is one that helps both sides in some way.
4. By giving up something of lesser value, you can sometimes gain something of a higher value.
5. You can't antagonize and persuade at the same time.

TO-DO LIST:

1. Consider the other side's probable positions as well as preparing your own.
2. Gather all the facts you can; there may be some specific information that can make or break you.
3. Don't start negotiating until you completely understand all the issues, and try to negotiate only one issue at a time.
4. Be prepared to fulfill at least some of the other side's needs.
5. Negotiate only with decision-makers; simply exchange information with others.
6. Start by listing the points of agreement.
7. Never tamper with the truth.

8. Be patient; speed usually means risk. For example, don't reveal your real deadline until you have to.

9. Don't let the other side set the tone or pace.

10. When you have to reject another person's idea, reject only the idea, not the person.

11. Take extreme stands only when they are sure to be advantageous.

12. Introduce an ultimatum near the end of a negotiation, never at the beginning.

13. If the other side introduces a deal-breaker early in the negotiation, put off discussing it in detail as long as you can.

14. Learn to master silence; it can be a powerful negotiating tool.

15. When you've reached the point where you have more to lose than to gain, stop negotiating.

IT TAKES
THREE YEARS TO
GROW ASPARAGUS

It's been said that there is no such thing as a perfectly patient person; there are only people who are very good at hiding their impatience. Even if that's the case, for ease of discussion I'll refer to the ability to disguise impatience as patience.

If you weren't born with patience, or the innate ability to hide your impatience, as the case might be, you're going to have to develop it, because patience succeeds more often than impulsiveness; we get the chicken by waiting for the egg to hatch, not by breaking it.

It's also not a very good idea to pull up a flower by its roots to see how it's doing. Which reminds me, did you know it takes three years to grow asparagus? Clearly, patience is an important quality in a successful asparagus grower. It's also an important ingredient of success in every facet of our daily lives.

It's not overstating the case to say that a moment of patience can avert a disaster and a moment of impatience can ruin a life. Consider the driver who runs a red light in order to save a couple of minutes and kills a child as a result of that moment of impatience. He's going to spend the rest of his life regretting that impulsive act. Now let's look at the less extreme, but still important, aspects of patience and impatience.

Patience is a subtle blend of wisdom and self-control. It often consists of simply doing something else in the meantime, such as reading in the doctor's waiting room, listening to a favourite CD when stuck in traffic, or gathering facts and carefully considering the pros and cons of a decision rather than rushing into an impulsive act.

Impatience can be a greater liability than inexperience. An inexperienced person who takes the time to properly analyze a situation and carefully consider the likely results of possible courses of action will make fewer mistakes than an experienced person who makes rash, poorly considered decisions.

Probably the most critical time to exercise patience is when you're angry. Patience in a moment of anger may save you days of regret. It might allow you to retain the services of a valued employee, the goodwill of an important customer, or the respect of your colleagues. It's particularly important to exercise patience with those who are less capable or less experienced than you are.

You will always encounter situations in which there's nothing to do but wait, such as being mired in traffic without your favourite CD, stuck in a long line somewhere, cooling your heels in a reception area without anything to read, or perhaps just waiting for an elevator. A great way to ease your frustration in these circumstances is to play "what if." Ask yourself *what* you would do *if* you found yourself in particular situations that could realistically arise at work, at home, or at play. You can also ask yourself *what* you would say *if* you were asked particular questions, or *if* you had to make a particular speech or presentation.

Two great benefits arise from playing "what if." First, you will avoid frustration while waiting, and second, if you some day actually find yourself in any of the imagined "what if" situations you will have a head start on dealing with it successfully.

There's no doubt that if you learn to be patient, your daily activities will go more smoothly and you'll be a happier person. That sounds like success by any measure.

REMEMBER:
1. A moment of patience can avert a disaster and a moment of impatience may ruin a life.
2. Patience is a subtle blend of wisdom and self-control.
3. Patience sometimes consists of simply doing something else in the meantime.
4. Impatience can be a greater liability than inexperience.

5. Patience in a moment of anger may avoid days of sorrow and regret.
6. Develop patience and you'll live a happier life.

TO-DO LIST:

1. Learn to disguise your impatience.
2. When there's nothing to do but wait, play "what if."

DOING SOMETHING ONCE DOESN'T MAKE YOU A PRO

It's obvious that a professional must have the requisite knowledge and skills to perform his job, so this chapter deals with the other characteristics that distinguish a professional from an amateur or a dilettante.

One of the most important of these distinguishing characteristics is the willingness to always make an extra effort. A number of years ago, I happened to be in the great pop singer Anne Murray's dressing room in Las Vegas just before her final performance of a lengthy engagement. She was rehearsing her hit song "Snowbird," a song she had sung thousands of times, and probably at least ten times that week. Yet she had felt that something wasn't quite right with the way she had sung it in her show earlier that evening. So there she was, with her guitar player, going over it again just before taking the stage.

Al MacInnis (no relation to the author), for many years an All-Star defenceman in the National Hockey League, and who had one of the hardest shots in the game, reputedly used to shoot a puck at least ten thousand times during the off-season.

Professionalism can't be bought, sold, inherited, or bequeathed. Professionalism is a personal attribute developed through a blend of knowledge, skill, hard work, and dedication of purpose. The hardest part about being a professional is not the successful performance of a single, difficult act, but rather the successful replication of it time and time again, day after day, year after year, in changing circumstances and under difficult demands. Doing something right once doesn't make you a professional any more than a random hole-in-one turns a duffer into a professional golfer.

Professionals strive to be at their best at all times. This includes how they look. Business professionals have to care about their appearances. You should always dress well and appropriately in any particular situation. An effective rule of thumb is to always dress just a little better than the occasion calls for, but always in the manner suited to the particular circumstances. The most respected business professionals are also usually well-groomed.

Another earmark of professionals is that they perform well even when they don't feel like it, whereas non-professionals often have difficulty achieving something even when they do feel like it. Professionals always operate on the basis that good enough is the enemy of best. No one would have blamed Columbus for turning back, but no one would have remembered him either.

Professionals keep their eyes on methods as well as on results. They're never afraid to try new things or to try doing old things in new ways. They'll always take the time to improve their craft, whether that entails intense study, extensive research, strenuous practice, or constant rehearsing.

REMEMBER:

1. There are requisites over and above knowledge and skills that a true professional must meet.
2. Professionals perform well even when they don't feel like it.
3. Professionals always operate on the basis that good enough is the enemy of best.

TO-DO LIST:

1. Always be willing to make an extra effort.
2. Dress just a little better than the occasion calls for but in a manner suited to the particular circumstances.
3. Be well-groomed.
4. Keep your eye on methods as well as on results.
5. Work hard at your craft.

EVERYBODY'S DAY HAS TWENTY-FOUR HOURS

You can read all the books and take all the courses there are that deal with time management (and there are plenty to choose from), but you'll find only one constant in effectively managing your time: everybody has the same twenty-four hours available every day. There's no such thing as one person having more time than another; some people are simply better at managing it. There's also no such thing as a one-size-fits-all system of time management. Time management is always personal. You can pick up some useful tips and insights from time management books and programs, even from this chapter, but no one else can manage your time for you. Effective and efficient use of your time is entirely up to you. Generally speaking, people tend to find the time to do the things they really want to do.

As mentioned elsewhere in this book, the strongest memory is weaker than the palest ink, so have a to-do list. Prioritize your to-do lists, always remembering that everything can't be a number-one priority and that your to-do list is not carved in stone. It can be changed, and should be changed if it's advantageous or necessary to do so. For example, when you get bogged down in a particularly difficult item, it's a good idea to pick one or two easier tasks and get a couple of successes behind you rather than sticking to the strict order of the list.

Never let the fact that you can't do everything you want to do keep you from doing what you can do. You can't do *everything* right now, but you can do *something* right now. Instead of wasting time lamenting the length of your list, prioritize an item and deal with it.

Each item on your list has to be done, delegated, or ditched. If it has to be done by you and you can't deal with it right now, then schedule a specific time later when you are going to deal with it. If the item can be delegated to someone else, then do so. It's usually best to delegate items that you don't like to do or that are weaknesses of yours, but be careful not to delegate them to someone for whom they are also weaknesses. Anything that you really can't do or delegate has to be ditched; not all tasks that we think we have to do really need to be done. Keeping an item on your to-do list that you're never going to get around to doing makes no more sense than keeping an item on the list that you will never be capable of doing.

Examine your habits; time is usually wasted in minutes, not hours. But a bucket with a tiny hole in the bottom will get just as empty as one with a hole you can put your fist through; it will just take a little longer. Keep track of your activities for a week to see where those minutes are slipping and adjust your activities accordingly. The only time you can really manage is right now. Take care of each day; let the calendar take care of the weeks, months, and years.

When establishing deadlines, base them on what you *can* do, not on what you'd *like* to do. Unrealistic deadlines are stressful and counterproductive to effective time management. You will usually achieve more by establishing a number of shorter deadlines for the various steps of a project than by having only one distant deadline for the whole job. And to ensure that you'll actually meet all those shorter deadlines, remember that they should be changed only when there's no other choice. When deadlines become negotiable, they become ineffective.

Probably the most common time management mistake is taking on more than you can realistically accomplish. If you're already busy, then you're going to have to drop an old activity before taking on a new one. You'll never be the consummate time manager until you learn to say "no." A polite no is always better than a broken promise.

Even after you've studied your habits to determine where you may be wasting time, continue to monitor your activities to be sure that you're doing what really is important rather than simply reacting to what seems urgent at that moment. There's usually a logical order in which things should be done should you wish to do them most efficiently, and when you disrupt that logic, time management suffers.

Don't fill your days with time-sensitive activities. If you do, you'll have no time to deal with unexpected emergencies. Nor will you have time to deal with unforeseen events that, although perhaps not qualifying as emergencies, still need to be dealt with, such as a distraught employee appearing in your office or a disgruntled client suddenly showing up in the reception area.

One of the most effective time management techniques is to do at least one thing every day that you don't want to do, and do it as early in the day as you can. Your to-do list will usually contain some distasteful chores, and getting rid of at least one of them early each day will have an incredibly positive effect on the quantity and quality of time at your disposal. There's a natural tendency to waste too much time thinking about the items that you are avoiding, which deters from both your effectiveness and maintaining healthy stress levels. Few things are as exhausting as an unfinished distasteful task. People who manage their time best and accomplish the most are those who don't wait to be in the mood; when something needs to be done, they do it.

Be sure tomorrow isn't the busiest day of the week. The best preparation for tomorrow is doing, to the best of your ability, today's work today.

REMEMBER:

1. People tend to find the time to do the things they really want to do.
2. Everything can't be a number-one priority.
3. All the items on your to-do list have to be done, delegated, or ditched.
4. To-do lists can be changed as circumstances warrant.
5. When deadlines become negotiable, they become ineffective.
6. A polite "no" is always better than a broken promise.
7. If you fill your days with time-sensitive activities, you'll have no time left to deal with emergencies.

TO-DO LIST:

1. Make to-do lists and follow them.
2. When you get bogged down, consider doing a couple of easier tasks to get a couple of successes behind you.
3. Don't let the fact that you can't do everything you want to do keep you from doing the things that you can do.
4. Examine your habits; time is usually wasted in minutes, not hours.

5. Take care of each day; let the calendar take care of the weeks, months, and years.

6. Base deadlines on what you can do, not on what you'd like to do.

7. Learn to say "no."

8. If you're already busy, drop an old activity before adding a new one.

9. Do what's really important rather than reacting to what simply seems urgent.

10. Do at least one thing every day that you don't want to do, and do it as early in the day as you can.

11. Be sure tomorrow isn't the busiest day of the week.

TAKE TIME TO THINK BUT NOT TO TREMBLE

You are never going to be worry-free; the best you can hope for is to be able to manage how your worries affect you. And you must learn to manage this; your health and well-being depend on it. Your success will also depend on how well you manage it, because every moment you spend worrying is a moment that's not contributing to your success.

Like time management, if there's a one-size-fits-all method for managing worry, I've never come across it. You're going to have to experiment to find out what methods work for you.

Here's what works for me. Worries that creep into my mind are usually things that I can do nothing about at the moment; therefore, taking time to worry is completely futile. So I make an appointment with myself to worry about the problem. I set aside a time in my mind (I don't enter the "appointment" in my diary), say fifteen minutes at 3:45 the next afternoon, during which I will worry much more effectively. If I catch myself worrying about the subject before the appointed time, I remind myself to put if off until then. What usually happens is that when 3:45 the next day rolls around, I've either forgotten about the problem or something more important is occupying my thoughts. In the rare instances when I do remember why I was so worried, I'll give it some thought as planned. Then one of two things usually happens: either my mind will wander off after a few seconds to something else, or I will actually come up with some ideas about how to deal with the situation.

Many people find that being busy is the best way to handle worry. The most effective method seems to be to do something that requires both physical and mental activity, such as playing a sport. Others hook up their iPod and go for a walk or a run. One friend of mine has a punching bag in his office and another bag in his basement at home. He finds that whenever worry threatens to become a problem, a few minutes pounding the bag work wonders.

There's a difference between being concerned about something and worrying about it. There are many things in life about which we should be concerned, but there's nothing about which we should be continually worried. A former mentor impressed this on me by pointing out that concern is *fore*thought whereas worry is *fear* thought. When you refuse to let your concern elevate itself to worry, you're more likely to come up with solutions to problems and ways to deal with difficulties, whereas worrying is counterproductive, a waste of time, and harmful to your health. I've heard it put this way: worry is when your stomach is firing bullets and your brain is firing blanks. When worry slips in, take time to think but not to tremble.

A lot of the worry in the world is caused by trying to make decisions before having enough information on which to base them. Instead of just stewing about a problem, follow the advice in Chapter 23 about making decisions. Take the time to consider what the causes of the problem are, what all the possible solutions are, what the best solution is likely to be, and what action you're going to take.

Another common mistake leading to unnecessary worry is the human tendency to read big implications into little facts. The odds are usually that whatever you're going through isn't as serious as it seems. If you're working on a way to handle a problem, there's nothing to be gained by worrying about it. When you're worried about something, you've probably already thought about the worst that can happen, but instead of stopping there, go on to think about what the odds actually are that the worst will come to pass, and then think about what you can do to improve the odds further yet.

Even the consequences of problems that can't be completely resolved can usually be greatly diminished by thinking calmly and deciding on a logical course of action. If you're capable of handling a situation, there's no need to worry about it. Look back on your life and you will find there have been a lot more worries than there were real dangers.

The depth of your worry will ultimately depend on the amount of time you spend thinking about it instead of getting busy and doing something about it. It's always better to do something about a problem rather than to just sit and fret.

The most senseless worry of all is worrying about something that you can't do anything about. Not only is it a waste of time, but worrying about things beyond your control will hamper your dealing with those that you *can* do something about. No matter which road you take, you're going to miss something, so don't waste time wishing you'd taken another one.

Never worry about what you've lost. Instead concentrate on what you have left and what you can do with that. Recognize that the occasional disappointment is part of life, and get on with it.

REMEMBER:

1. You're never going to be worry-free, but you can learn to manage it.
2. There's no one-size-fits-all solution for managing worry.
3. Physical and mental activities help manage worry.

4. Worry is when your stomach is firing bullets and your brain is firing blanks.

5. A lot of worry is caused by trying to make decisions before having enough information on which to base them.

6. There are a lot more worries than there are real dangers.

7. It's always better to do something about a situation than it is to worry about it.

8. Worrying about things that you can't control will adversely affect those that you can.

9. No matter which road you take, you're going to miss something; don't waste time wishing you'd taken another one.

TO-DO LIST:

1. Experiment until you find out what worry management techniques work best for you and then utilize them.

2. Recognize the difference between concern and worry.

3. Don't read big implications into little facts. If you're capable of handling a situation, there's no need to worry about it.

4. Recognize that the occasional disappointment is part of life, and get on with it.

31
TEN FINAL PRECEPTS

As mentioned in the Introduction, this book is based entirely on what I've learned during my career through advising, listening to, being around, and observing very successful people from all walks of life.

Over the years, I recorded my observations in note form in a huge binder that I call "A Collection of Wisdoms." Following is a list of ten of these wisdoms, precepts really, that, although they didn't fit seamlessly into any of the book's chapters, are by themselves very important in achieving success.

The elements of success discussed in the foregoing chapters will vary in importance depending on your particular circumstances at any given time. But the following wisdoms constitute a general code of conduct impervious to time, place, or circumstances. Making them a part of your everyday pursuits will contribute enormously to your success, your overall quality of life, and your happiness.

- To get anywhere, you have to start from where you are.

- Improving what you have is more productive than longing for something that you can't have.

- What one thing, if you did it well, would have a positive effect on your life? Why aren't you doing it?

- If an activity adds to your life, continue it. If it doesn't, drop it.

- One loving act is worth a thousand wonderful sentiments. When you think of a nice thing to do for someone, do it. When you have a kind thought, express it.

- When people are kept waiting, they will always be less pleasant to deal with. Think for a moment about the signals you send by being late. You're telling other people that
  - a) you're more important than they are;
  - b) the things you have to do are more important than the things they have to do;
  - c) you're not very well organized;
  - d) you're irresponsible;
  - e) you're insensitive to their feelings;
  - f) all of the above.

- Be the kind of person others would like to see even when they don't feel like seeing someone.

- If you're intelligent and you're bored, it's your fault.

- When you think you're all-powerful, try ordering someone else's dog around.
- When you stop learning, you start to die.

ACKNOWLEDGEMENTS

Sincere thanks to the folks at Random House Canada, especially Anne Collins, for her faith in the project, and Craig Pyette, who understands that editing means improving a manuscript, not just changing it. Further thanks to Kathryn Exner and Gillian Watts respectively, who copy edited and proofread the manuscript.